RAW FAITH

Fr. Pete!

Blessing -

Also by Marilyn Sewell

ANTHOLOGIES

Cries of the Spirit
Claiming the Spirit Within
Resurrecting Grace
Breaking Free: Women of Spirit at Midlife and Beyond

NONFICTION

Wanting Wholeness, Being Broken
Threatened with Resurrection
A Little Book on Forgiveness
A Little Book on Prayer
A Little Book of Reflections
Unitarian Universalist Culture: the Present and the Promise

FILM

Marilyn is the subject of a documentary film, *Raw Faith*, directed by Peter Weidensmith. See the trailer at www.marilynsewell.com.

For more information visit
WWW.MARILYNSEWELL.COM

RAW FAITH

Following the Thread

🐚 A MEMOIR 🐚

by Marilyn Sewell

FULLER PRESS
PORTLAND · OREGON

Praise for
Raw Faith: Following the Thread

Raw Faith: Following the Thread will challenge and inspire. Marilyn Sewell writes with an alluring style and a candor that lives up to the "raw" in the book's title. A remarkable story of a person overcoming pain and abandonment to give so much to others in need of encouragement and uplift.

> – Tom Krattenmaker, *USA Today Board*
> *of Contributors*

There is a Zen saying: "If you are lucky, your heart will break." This is the story of a young girl's mother loss and search for home, ending in a courageous woman's great public ministry of healing and passion, then in the grace of a late life love story. Her spiritual courage and sense of calling is the thread that runs throughout. Written in luminous lines, her story can, if you are open yourself, help to break *you* open to the raw human faith that will guide you, through your own maze, to greater wholeness and compassion.

> – John Buehrens, Former President, Uni-
> tarian Universalist Association

At what proves to be a fulcrum in Marilyn Sewell's life, her creative writing teacher—the remarkable Wendell Berry—challenges her to "Tell the truth about what you know. That's all." And in this moving memoir, Sewell does indeed tell her truth, her fascinating and at times harrowing personal history. Candid, witty, compelling, this is the story of her long and arduous search for home, a place that isn't—as she tells us—a *place* at all. A true home is "a condi-tion of the spirit." In *Raw Faith* she leads us—her grateful readers—with her, on her odyssey toward that transcendent state.

> – Paulann Petersen, Oregon Poet Laureate

"I am a called person," says Marilyn Sewell. "On some level I have known that all of my life." Her calling follows her through growing up southern and female in the 1950s, discovering the women's movement a decade later; through a marriage that fails not with arguments but with silences; through unsuccessful flirtations with Catholic and Baptist churches as she tries to ground her faith, finally discovering Unitarians, and finding the fit so strong that she goes on to study at the Starr King School for the Ministry and eventually finds her calling at the First Unitarian Church in Portland, Oregon. Her non-linear journey makes for an engaging read because Sewell is a talented writer, bringing a novelist's gifts for description and characterization. Her memoir was written as a companion piece to the documentary film about her of the same name but this book does not depend on it and stands alone very well as an incredible woman's reflections on an incredible journey.

> – Charles Deemer, award-winning author, teacher, and former editor of *Oregon Literary Review*

This deeply personal memoir is moving and redemptive. Marilyn Sewell tells her story with great candor and insight.

> – Sharon Salzberg, author of *Real Happiness at Work*

"There's a thread you follow," says William Stafford in the poem that opens Marilyn Sewell's wise and wonderful memoir, *Raw Faith*.

If, like me, you often struggle to see that thread in your own life, you'll find comfort and inspiration in Sewell's courageous story. Her willingness to follow a thread she cannot always see, and to open herself to love, and beauty, in a world of pain and uncertainty reminds us what faith really means. Sewell is a wonderful writer, thanks perhaps to the instruction she received from Wendell Berry, to "tell the truth about what you know." I for one am deeply grateful for her story, her honesty, her wisdom and her example as a writer. Highly recommended.

– Marianne Elliott, author of *Zen Under Fire: How I Found Peace in the Midst of War*

This book is a woman's odyssey. It begins with the story of an earnest and serious girl whose father takes her away from her mother and lodges her and her brother and sister at his parents' home in a small town in Louisiana. Here in the midst of family violence, alcoholism and the brokenness of divorce, and feeling herself an outsider, even an outcast, Marilyn trains herself at an astonishingly young age to listen for her own truth and to stand up for it. (At one point she defies the Catholic priest and his threats of fire and brimstone if she dares to leave the Church, which she does!) Told with candor, unflinching honesty and courage, Marilyn traces the steps and painful missteps of her life as she struggles to find her calling. For anyone striving to live an authentic life, amidst the wreckage of childhood or not, the story of this courageous and determined woman will be an inspiration.

– Dianne Stepp, author of *Half-Moon of Clay*

When a writer can make you laugh and cry at the same time, you know you're in gentle, skilled, compassionate hands. Marilyn Sewell is such a writer, chronicling the intimate experience of a woman's life in her memoir, *Raw Faith*. Read it, let it touch and inspire you.

— Sandy Boucher, author of *Dancing in the Dharma*

Marilyn Sewell's memoir takes us directly into paradoxes that we all sense but seldom articulate—that life can be lived both spontaneously and reflectively, that our heart-wrenching failures need not defeat us, that our deepest intentions, not religious institutions, can ultimately redeem us.

— Charles Suhor, Ph.D., former Deputy Director, National Council of Teachers of English

In Memorium

Melissa Buchan
a true friend, still missed after all these years

Acknowledgements

I MUST BEGIN BY THANKING RON LOEWINSOHN, MY WISE AND PATIENT teacher at the University of California at Berkeley, who advised me on an early draft of this book. It appears here with substantial changes. Susan Griffin read and commented upon portions of the original text and encouraged me as a writer. Katie Radditz read several drafts, giving helpful suggestions. I am grateful to Barbara Dills, who offered valuable suggestions as to content and format during my final year of writing, as well as giving me support and advice as I struggled with form.

My deepest gratitude goes to my husband, George Crandall, extraordinary critic of my work, and my greatest advocate and sustainer.

The Way It Is

There's a thread you follow. It goes among
things that change. But it doesn't change.
People wonder about what you are pursuing.
You have to explain about the thread.
But it is hard for others to see.
While you hold it you can't get lost.
Tragedies happen; people get hurt
or die; and you suffer and get old.
Nothing you do can stop time's unfolding.
You don't ever let go of the thread.

– William Stafford

Preface

IN THESE PAGES YOU WILL ENCOUNTER A PROFOUNDLY MOVING SPIRITUAL memoir written by an extraordinary woman. For 17 years Marilyn Sewell served as the pastor of the First Unitarian Church in Portland, Oregon. When she began her tenure in 1992, the church, which was founded in 1877 was the preferred place of worship for the city's most elite and prominent citizens. A respected institution, with an impressive record of charitable efforts, it had close to 675 members. Yet despite many achievements in the past and a comfortable status quo, under Sewell's leadership a great deal was to change. By the time she stepped down in 2009, the congregation had swelled to 1500, becoming the best attended church in the denomination. In great part, this dramatic rise in membership can be attributed to the radical shift in the church's agenda that Sewell initiated, encouraged and supported. Starting in the first months of her ministry, as Portland was fighting over gay and lesbian rights, when members of the church put up a red band around the block that read "Hate Free Zone," First Unitarian steadily gained a reputation for speaking out about social and economic justice and taking a strong stand against war. As some parishioners describe the change, this house of worship became a "people's church," inviting in and speaking for everyone, including and even especially those whom society has marginalized.

But it was not just courageous stands nor was it the numerous programs that supported the community and encouraged religious education which were organized with Sewell's guidance that made this church so attractive to so many. Something else happened with her ministry that is more difficult and yet equally important to describe here. Though her sermons expressed feelings that a great many in the community shared, that was not all they did. As one long-standing member of the church, Cindy Cumfer, puts it, "they changed something in me that was not my mind." Something in Marilyn's presence, the sound of her voice, the authenticity of her feeling, the honesty that lay behind her words touched Cumfer so deeply that she made the decision to place her spirituality at the center of her life.

Many members of her congregation have noted the way that during services Marilyn seemed to be able to put aside her ego. The same ability is manifest in this memoir but in a wholly different way. This book is not about her ministry but her path to it and the very human difficulties she encountered in the world and in herself along the way. Rather than portray herself as the mature and wiser soul she was to become, she gives us moving accounts of the loneliness, anger, dismay, and desolation she suffered on her way to her ministry. Neither a compendium of wisdom, an outline of doctrine, nor even a description of how we should live, this memoir describes the vulnerability and confusion Sewell felt as daily she struggled to find meaning and connection in her life

Though along the way, we come to understand the origins of Sewell's passion for social justice, including her concern for women's and civil rights, the book does not proselytize us about any belief or cause. And though it is very revealing, unlike Augustine's famous spiritual memoir, the author does not confess sins. Nor, as with the work St John of the Cross nor Julian of Norwich, does this book restrict itself to what are usually considered to be spiritual conflicts. Depicting the daily grit of survival and the troubling life of relationships, this book reads more like a novel, engaging us in the life of a woman with whom we can identify because we recognize her dilemmas and her hopes as being like our own. It is, in short, a people's memoir.

In this sense too, if not the first, this book is certainly among the first really modern spiritual memoirs. The editor of a remarkable volume of poetry by women called *Cries of the Spirit* and author of several other volumes, Marilyn Sewell is a skilled writer and this makes her narrative vivid with detail and wit, not to mention the music of her prose. But something else of another order is operating here too, what one of her congregation noted as her "ability to turn over to something larger." A transformational art, all the more remarkable in this volume because she has chosen to depict the vicissitudes of every day life. She does not categorize her struggles as either sinful or saintly, but treats them instead as both earthly and spiritual at the same time. Thus the book you are about to read is not only inspiring but revolutionary, if only because here the divine is constantly discovered and rediscovered in the ordinary, neither as redemption nor condemnation, but simply as a dimension that belongs to all existence.

Susan Griffin, Berkeley, 2014

🌿

CHAPTER 1

in which I lose Mother

I REMEMBER THE DAY WE LEFT.

We were living in Cincinnati, in a two-story white house across the street from Holy Name School. Big Papa and Uncle Gene drove up to our house one day in July. Mother wasn't home. Daddy spread a sheet on the floor, pulled out drawers, and dumped our clothes inside. Then he tied the sheet up and threw it in the back end of Big Papa's black Studebaker. I remember that car had a running board.

We couldn't take my puppy, Daddy said. We could just take the clothes. Not my big bride doll, either.

We all crowded into the car and Uncle Gene drove us fast, out of Cincinnati, into the countryside, across the river on a small railroad bridge with no rails, on across the state line to Kentucky, on towards Louisiana.

I left a room of my own and my own bed with my patent leather shoes neatly tucked under. I left my "box of secrets" in its hiding place. I was nine years old. I didn't see my mother again until I graduated from college.

🌿

We children were not told where our mother was or why she became so absolutely absent from our lives. Later we learned she had been sent to a mental hospital. We didn't ask about her, and now I wonder why. Perhaps we sensed from our father's troubled eyes that the past was best left behind. Reasoning that things were the way they were because of some kind of unspoken necessity, we followed blindly, trusting our caretakers, as children are wont to do. But of course a mother cannot be left behind. *Something is missing! What is it?* I always felt awkward and unfinished, unworthy of love, suspicious of affection offered. My mother's absence became a great presence in my life.

CHAPTER 2

in which I come to live in a strange house

I can't remember Mother's face. Only six months, and the face is already lost. I'm lying in bed beside my little sister Donna, who is sleeping soundly. I hear the Frigidaire humming, a lone dog howling, my grandfather snoring from the room across the hall.

Sitting up, I see the room and its contents clearly, for the moon gives light through the row of windows facing my bed, illuminating the space. I don't belong here. The room is a dining room and not a bedroom. Our bed has been shoved into one corner. I am staying here at Granny and Big Papa's for just a while, I think. But I'm not going back to Mother, Daddy says, so maybe I am here for good. I don't know.

Why did Daddy take us? Why would he leave Mother? He never really said, except that Mother was sick and couldn't take care of us children, and so we just had to leave. I wish that somebody would tell me what happened. But no one talks about the move, ever.

On the wall to my left, I see the mahogany china cabinet, where the good dishes are kept. In the bottom drawer Granny keeps her own special slips and nightgowns, in case she ever gets sick and has to go decent to the hospital, she says. I look at the sideboard, where the serving dishes and the sterling silver are kept, and then at the big dining table, dark and shining, surrounded by six massive chairs.

I can't remember Mother's face. Let's see, she has dark hair, darker than my own, and she is tall, I think. I see her now in the kitchen, the way she used to be in her apron. Her back is to me, I call her, and she turns and—her face is gone! I can't make it out anymore, no matter how I try. I wish I could remember her face, or her eyes at least.

⁂

Pastries. We used to have pastries for breakfast. Mother would get up early every morning and go to the bakery and bring back flat cakes, oozing blackberry and cherry fillings, with whipped cream on top. I would hear her come in, the door slam, and a bit later the coffee smell would drift up to my room as I lay in bed, only half-awake. Then Jim and Donna and I and Mother, too, would all eat the cakes. We would have milk with ours, and she would have coffee.

I can almost see her face now: her brown bright eyes and her red mouth, her lipstick coming off on the paper napkin from the bakery, as she wipes the sticky whipped cream off her mouth. I lick my lips, and almost taste the breakfast cake again.

Mother sang me to sleep in the rocking chair. She sang me a song about soldiers—something, let's see—"little soldier's had a busy day," that's it, that's the end. Her voice was deep, low for a mommy. She stroked my hair, I think. Yes, I think she did stroke my hair and my face when she rocked me. I would be almost asleep, and she would carry me to bed and tuck my blue blanket close round me. And I think she kissed me then. Probably she did. *But what did her face look like?*

I am tired but not sleepy. Something from the kitchen calls to me, no not from the kitchen, something inside of me calls me to the kitchen and I obey without thinking, I tip-toe out of bed, my feet cold on the wooden floor. Pulling my skimpy gown round me, I feel like an intruder. I hardly breathe. As I move, another part of me stands outside myself and wonders at the courage of the child who is herself, and yet fears for her in this strange house that she knows, surely, is not her own.

Water. Water would taste good, I think. The full moon floods light through the window, onto the white porcelain sink and black cabinet tops and the black-and-white checkered linoleum floor. I see just one at first, a large black roach, a water bug Granny calls them, an inch or more long, feeding on the cabinet top, feeding on a scrap of food, waving its long antennae at me. I look away, and I see another crawling into the potato bin, where the potatoes are sprouting, rotten, useless, and I smell their sweet decay. Another squeezes its length slowly, slowly between the cabinet and the wall and slips out of sight, and still another runs across the floor in front of me as I jump back. I know that the place is full of them, mostly hidden in daylight hours but all the night crawling their blackness over the canned soups and vegetables, inside the flour and sugar and pancake mix, circling inside the drinking glasses and cups. Now they're out, a dozen at least in view, feeding in the kitchen sink, on the crumbs on the floor, crawling right now perhaps in the very glass I was to drink from.

I hear a scream and another and another and only when Big Papa is there with his cane and my little brother Jim is there and Granny in her long gown from the front room do I know that it is I myself who is screaming and screaming and somehow I still cannot stop and I feel myself being shaken and hear a command STOP IT, STOP IT and my name called, MARILYN JANE I SAID STOP IT, WHAT'S WRONG WITH YOU CHILD, STOP IT NOW, STOP IT NOW, MARILYN, MARILYN, MARILYN, STOP IT! And I stop hearing the scream inside me and outside me the scream stops, too, and I look around at Big Papa's hard face and Granny without her teeth, looking strange, and I see Jim is scared, and Big Papa says, We're not going to have tantrums like this, Marilyn Jane, in this house, this behavior has got to stop. I try to tell about the roaches, which are all gone now in the light of the kitchen, but Big Papa grabs my shoulder and says, Don't talk back to me, girl! I said I am not going to stand for behavior like this, do you hear? And I nod and nod and stop my crying.

Everybody goes back to bed, and my body twitches, twitches

for a while, and I cry for a long time, holding the pillow tightly and soaking it wet with my tears, but making no sound, for fear of waking someone again.

At last the shuddering of my body stops, and I give myself to sleep. Fluttering wings, angels' wings, surround me in my dreams and lift me, weightless, to float without care, far above the earth. It is a sleep that I have not known for a long time, a deep blue and purple sleep which, like an ocean, covers me and comforts me and heals me sufficient to wake another day.

CHAPTER 3

in which I grow up Southern

OUR NEW HOME WAS WITH GRANNY AND BIG PAPA, OR JUST PAPA, AS WE sometimes called him. They lived in Homer, Louisiana, a town of "5,000 Friendly People"—or so said the sign at the city limits. Homer was a typical small Southern community with a white Georgian courthouse in the center of the town square. The courthouse was surrounded by a plush green lawn of St. Augustine grass, on which stood a statue of a Confederate soldier.

Of Homer's 5,000 inhabitants, 2,000 were white and 3,000 black. Blacks lived on the outskirts of town in "Niggertown." Their houses were wooden shacks built on boulders as foundation, and instead of glass, tarpaper covered the windows. The women worked as cooks and housecleaners in the homes of the whites, and the men worked in the fields. Every white family except the very poorest had "help." We paid our cook ten dollars a week.

On the street around the courthouse in Homer were shops: Jitney Jungle, where we got our groceries; Marinsky's Clothing, owned by the only Jewish family in town; White's Dry Goods, where Miss Altalene, my Sunday School teacher worked; the Homer National Bank, where Joe Chrisler, a quiet banker and our neighbor, committed suicide; a fire station, and a drug store. There was a movie theater, where I saw science fiction movies like *The Thing* and *The Creature from the Black Lagoon*, various werewolf movies, cowboy movies, and the occasional drama: Rock Hudson and Jennifer Jones in *A Farewell to Arms*.

7

Movies and books introduced me to a world larger than Homer. I went to the town library every Saturday, and checked out the allowed number of volumes. The library was one large room decorated with the heads of various jungle animals that had been killed by one of the town fathers: lion, rhino, gazelle, wildebeest. I read *Gone with the Wind* and *Marjorie Morningstar,* along with all the teen romances like *Practically Seventeen,* by Rosamond du Jardin. I read autobiographies of people who overcame obstacles to rise to greatness: Lincoln, George Washington Carver, Amelia Earhart.

My grandparents lived in a white frame house, set under a gigantic oak tree, about a ten-minute walk from town. The street was Fulmer Street, named after my grandfather, who had been the postmaster at one time. Like most homes in the South, this one had a front porch, where the family members rocked and fanned and drank iced tea during the summer. The lawn was broad and covered with the same St. Augustine grass that surrounded the courthouse, thick and soft under foot, and cool in the summer. Rows of nandina bushes with their shiny green leaves and bright red berries grew around the front porch, and in the spring there were tulips and daffodils and iris in the flowerbeds near the garage.

The back yard had a chicken coop with fat hens that clucked and waddled and pecked in the dust and gave eggs every day. The rest of the back and side yards were used for a vast garden out of which came every kind of vegetable known to grow in the area: potatoes, onions, tomatoes, yellow squash, purple-hull peas, lima beans, green beans, okra, asparagus, turnip greens, mustard, plus cantaloupe and sometimes watermelon. My grandfather turned the soil each spring with a wooden push-plow and a mule, the sweat pouring off his thin body, his string undershirt clinging to his frame. There was a green apple tree at the right side of the house, for pies. Fig trees and blackberry vines gave us preserves for biscuits.

This semi-rural setting offered its own kind of abundance and constancy—no one ever moved from the neighborhood while we lived there. Although my father's parents, then in their 70's, did not entirely appreciate their wayward son and his three children dropping in on them permanently, in the South you do not turn kin away, so my grandparents made room. I wonder now at their generosity in taking us children in, the youngest only three years old. It couldn't have been easy.

Daddy and my little brother Jim slept in the small back bedroom, off the back yard, shaded by a black walnut tree. My sister Donna and I slept in the dining room. The dining table and chairs were never moved, nor was the chest of drawers or the buffet table. A bed was simply stuck in the corner, a hanger attached to the back of the door for our clothes. Until Aunt Mellie gave Donna and me a little blue chest of drawers, I folded our underwear and placed it on the dining table. This arrangement continued for fifteen years, until Donna graduated from high school and left home.

The house had one small bathroom, which held a washing machine, besides the usual contrivances. The bathroom was a much-coveted space, not just because all six of us needed to use the toilet and bathe there, but because it was the only room in the house that had a lock. There I could be alone. And the bathroom was warm in the winter, for it had a small gas heater. The only other room that was heated was Big Papa's bedroom, which doubled as the TV room.

We three children did not think of ourselves deprived—things were simply the way they were. We did not question our father's decision to take us from our mother. He did it, so it must have been right. No one told us that Mother was in a mental hospital. No one told us why she didn't call or write for a year. No one told us that after she got out of the hospital, she went to a lawyer to try to get her children back. That was a useless endeavor, since no judge in Louisiana would have considered our mother's petition.

When she was released from the hospital, Mother continued to live in Cincinnati, in an apartment owned by her brother Buddy. She made her living cleaning houses for wealthy Jewish people, who were kind to her: Goldbergs, Rosenthals.

Calling occasionally, usually when she had had too much beer to drink, she would rant in a slurred voice about the Fulmers and how they took her children away. She wrote letters in her strong, passionate script: *"How are you, how is school going, it's snowing here . . .",* often enclosing a few dollars. Tearing open the letters, I looked for the money, not caring about the message, wishing this sad, angry woman were not my mother.

Gifts came regularly on birthdays and at Christmas. I would open a crumpled white box from Shillito's department store, tied with cheap pink ribbon. The frilly clothes, all ruffles and bows, seemed to have been bought for some other child, for some imagined daughter, not for the tall, thin, angular girl I was becoming. My mother didn't know me at all.

Mother's maiden name was Marion Denterlein. I don't know whether or not she had a middle name. Her parents were Arthur and Katherine Denterlein, long divorced, both of whom lived in Cincinnati. Katherine, known as Kay, ran a large boarding house on Auburn Avenue. She was a wizened little German woman with a sour smell always about her, who ate pickled pigs feet, drank Geritol, and reclined on a sofa in a darkened room most of the day. She arose only to give orders for something she wanted done. My grandfather, a pasty-faced man with a limp who spat tobacco juice, couldn't be trusted with girl children.

My mother studied ballet as a child. I have no idea who noticed her talent or encouraged her. I have pictures of her in her ballet costume, on her toes, her arms outspread, like some lovely winged creature. Using the name Marion Denton, she left home at the tender age of thirteen to go on the stage; she danced with a troop of girls all over the United States and Canada during the 1930's. The accounts of her life on the road are vague and lacking in detail. What gave her the courage to leave home at such an early age, and go into the sophisticated and worldly scene of entertainment? Or more to the point, why did she flee from her home at such an early age?

When hard economic times came and the dancing stopped,

Mother found employment selling Goody hair curlers in Washington, D.C. She ate lunch most days in a German restaurant called the Old Heidelberg, where she was spotted by a handsome young waiter, James Fulmer, who had come from Louisiana to find work. He courted her, and they fell in love. My favorite picture shows them sitting together on a park bench, Mother with a ribbon in her dark hair, and a wide smile, Daddy handsome and pleased with himself. He thought she was gorgeous and sexy. I can tell by the way he looks at her in the early snapshots. She thought he was charming and fun. I know this because she told me so. I was their first child, of three, born in 1941.

Shortly after my birth, my mother had what they called then "a nervous breakdown," the first of three, one after each child. Now her illness would be identified as postpartum depression and would be treated, but then there was little knowledge and less help. She managed to get herself and her new baby to Cincinnati, where she had the support of her mother and an extended family. I was cared for by Aunt Florence, mother's brother's wife, who once told me that my mother was so distraught after my birth that I would cry every time I was brought near her.

Where was my father at the time? Did he continue to work in Washington, D.C., or did he come with her to Cincinnati? I don't know. So much is gone, never to be recovered. My family history is like an intricate tabletop puzzle, with so many pieces missing, so many gaps, that it's hard to make the connections that would yield any kind of whole picture. Motives, sequences, whole relationships and some relatives are simply missing.

CHAPTER 4

in which we celebrate Christmas

Donna still believes in Santa Claus, even though she is already six. You would think that the kids at school would have told her by now, but no, she is still a believer, so she is pushing at my shoulder, whispering in my ear, trying to wake me at 5:00 a.m. I put her off until around 7:00, then reach for my chenille robe and drag my shivering body out of bed. My feet are cold on the wooden floor, and I can't find my slippers. *If she doesn't find out soon, I'm going to tell her myself.*

Jim comes in next—he is looking for a bicycle this year. Then Granny and Papa shuffle in. Daddy is still in bed, wouldn't you know—being drunk on Christmas Eve doesn't set you up so well for Christmas Day. But Donna keeps after him, shaking him and pulling the covers down. I hear her in the back bedroom, Come on. Come on, Daddy. Get up. Come on, right now. She won't let go, that girl. Daddy finally makes his way down the hall, stubbled face, eyes still red and swollen. Let's open the presents now! Donna cries. Sister, you hand them out. She doesn't know I just wrapped them and put them under the tree a few hours earlier.

So I read the tags and hand out the colorful boxes, one by one. Big Papa gives us kids what he gives us every year—a shiny new silver dollar. He always chuckles and says, Now don't spend all this in one place. I don't know why he thinks this is funny. He gives Granny a bird statue. She has dozens of them, inside cupboards, on mantels and shelves, and now here is another one. A finch, it looks like, and ugly as sin.

Jim gets his bicycle. I bought it at the hardware store last week. I couldn't wrap it, so I just propped it up against the wall next to the tree. Donna gets a red wagon, which I couldn't wrap either, but I did fix up the doll she wanted in a box that doesn't look like a doll box, so she is super surprised when she opens that one. Daddy gets a lunch box, as usual. He loses his every year, and so every Christmas, he gets a new one. You'd think he didn't want one, seeing as how he can't keep up with it. He always acts like he's surprised, and like it's just what he wanted all along.

I get a heart bracelet from Daddy. I told him ahead of time that I wanted a bracelet, but I had in mind a charm bracelet that jangled, that's what all the kids were wearing. This is a real gold bracelet, with an expandable arm band, and a plate with two hearts entwined on the front, with one of my initials engraved in each heart. I don't want to hurt his feelings, but the last thing I wanted was a heart bracelet from my own daddy. So I tell him how much I like it and all, but the truth is, I will never wear it. It would be too embarrassing. It's like your daddy is your boyfriend, or something.

Pretty soon all the aunts and uncles and cousins begin arriving—Uncle Lemos and Aunt Sugar and my three stuck-up cousins from Baton Rouge, Uncle Varnel and Aunt Frances trailing in from Texas, and Aunt Bernadine and Uncle Marinus, all the way from Washington State. Uncle Marinus is from Holland and grows bulbs—that's why we have so many tulips and daffodils in the spring. Uncle Gene and Aunt Louise and their kids Jesse Charles and Johnny and Little Louise come in—they live just up the road in Arcadia. And Aunt Mellie is always there, she's from Haynesville, fourteen miles north. At Christmas, the house is not an old folks' house anymore—kids' feet are running up and down the hall, and turkey and dressing smells start coming from the kitchen. The men gather in the living room, telling jokes and stories. They drink cups of strong coffee laced with chicory. The smoke from their pipes and cigarettes drifts down the hall.

I listen in on their talk sometimes. That's how I learned about

Big Papa, how his father was a Baptist preacher who beat him and then threw him out of the house and left him on his own when he was sixteen.

I also learned about Uncle Bill, Big Papa's brother. It seems that Uncle Bill was just fourteen years old and there at the family farm in Texas all by himself one day when a man rode up to collect a debt. Uncle Bill told him to get off the property. When he refused, Uncle Bill shot and killed him. In that day and time Texas justice could be swift and sure, so the family packed up and left, on the spot. That's how come the Fulmers are from Louisiana and not Texas.

I never found out anything more about Uncle Bill, except that he supposedly married five times. I figured he must have been long dead by the time we came to Homer. He was kind of like a myth, or a family legend, not a real person. But last year my brother Jim went to a Fulmer reunion and met a daughter of Uncle Bill's. She said all the time we were growing up in Homer, Uncle Bill lived in Haynesville. Aunt Mellie, my daddy's sister, and her daughter and son-in-law and their children lived in Haynesville, too, but no one ever let on that Uncle Bill was there, never said a word about him. How could a family member be disowned this way, completely forgotten, wiped out of existence? He must have been a major black sheep. My father filled that role for the next generation.

⁂

The women are crisscrossing the kitchen in each other's paths, preparing the dinner. Besides the turkey and cornbread dressing, there are sweet potatoes with marshmallows, green beans, lime jello salad with whipped cream and pineapple and pecans, mashed potatoes, cranberry sauce, homemade sweet pickles, fresh hot yeast rolls and butter, and of course both mincemeat and pumpkin pies for dessert. The same every year. My aunts laugh and giggle as they work, elbowing each other, telling jokes about men. Sometimes they laugh themselves out of breath, and their eyes fill with tears at their own silliness. I am underfoot, I know, but I want to stay. I love to hear their talk and their laughter. I feel safe when they are here. So I run little errands and keep the mixing bowls and pots and pans washed as we go along.

I keep thinking about Daddy. He won't start drinking again 'til dark, I know. But he is in for a surprise this year. I searched out his bottle high up in the rafters of the garage. Standing on a box, I stretched my arm as far as I could to get the whiskey down. A fifth of Old Crow, it was, and nearly full. I decided then and there to get rid of it—poured it right into the daffodil bed. I felt guilty all the while I poured, it was like pouring out money, I knew, it was such a waste, and I'm told fifty times a day not to waste anything, but I don't want Daddy drunk again tonight. I bet he'll never say anything to me, but he'll know who poured out his whiskey.

Dinnertime comes about four o'clock, and we all gather in the breakfast room. Aunt Bernadine gave Granny sterling silver and china years ago— she is the rich aunt from Washington State—and we bring it out every Thanksgiving and Christmas. The big table is glimmering just like a picture in a magazine for ladies. There is a child's table, too, set with the regular silver and everyday plates. That's where I sit. So does Daddy. I think he wants it that way, because he eats at the child's table year after year.

Big Papa sits at the head of the big table, of course, and he is the one who says the blessing. This is the only bad part of the meal, to have to hear Papa's blessing. In the first place, it is going to be a long one, and in the second place, it is going to make the rest of us feel guilty and him look good. The way he says grace always makes me feel that I have no business taking up space in the world and breathing air.

I especially hate it when he uses big words that I don't under-stand, as if he is going to impress God. Like this Christmas. After he gets through thanking God for "all our multitudinous and boun-teous blessings" and asking forgiveness for those "poor lost sinners," among which he clearly does not number himself, he finishes off by asking that "we all might walk more circumspectly with Thee."

How can he pray like this? I know how he treats folks every day. How he orders Granny around like she is his slave. Some more coffee, Mama, he will say. Or, Is this all the cornbread? And she will get up for the umpteenth time and go patiently into the kitchen for whatever he wants. Never mind that she has just cooked it, and is dead tired. If we are short on meat, you can be sure that he takes his share first, and gets the best that's there. And Lord help us if we kids think something is funny during dinner. Maybe he thinks laughter will make the milk curdle.

The only thing worse than hearing Big Papa pray is hearing Daddy pray. Although Daddy is generally considered too unworthy to pray, sometimes for some unknown reason, Papa will ask him to. James, will you say the blessing, please, Papa says out of the blue, and I feel a chill coming on. Daddy has sinful ways, Big Papa says, and he reminds us kids of that from time to time. Drinking and carousing around. Not coming home at night. Going off to see women. Gambling—or giving away—his money.

Daddy *knows* he is in trouble with the Lord. And big trouble at that.

When Papa asks Daddy to pray, it is always the same. Daddy hangs his head low and is silent for a long time. Then great big tears ease their way out of the corners of his eyes, and he tries to cover his face with one hand, and he prays, Forgive me, God, for being a low-down, dirty, rotten sinner. Amen. His praying always make my eyes fill up, too, in spite of myself.

But mainly I am embarrassed. That's not what a blessing ought to be. I don't want to think of my father as low-down, dirty, and rotten, and I don't want him to think of himself that way. If he is so set on sinning I wish he'd just do it and quit apologizing for it. Besides, if he is a no-good sinner, then somebody else has to be in charge of the family honor, and that somebody turns out to be me.

CHAPTER 5

in which I get Mama Dog

IN HOMER, LOUISIANA, EVERYBODY HAD A DOG. SOME WERE HUNTING dogs, and could point and flush out birds, like the dogs raised by my Uncle Gene, but mostly people had pets—no fancy breeds, just mongrels. These animals didn't get dog food out of a bag or a can—dogs ate table scraps. There was no such thing as a leash law. As one farm boy noted, "I don't understand these city folks putting a rope on their dogs and following them around to watch them shit." That pretty much says it. The dogs had the run of the neighborhood, and just as we knew all our neighbors, we also knew their dogs.

We had Mama-dog, who was more my dog than anybody else's. She was always waiting for me after school. As is the way with dogs, she loved me unconditionally, the only exception being my practice sessions with my coronet, which I started playing in the eighth grade. She would howl in the most mournful way, turn her tail under, and slink away as I played.

This is how we got her. Rain had been falling for the better part of three days. It was one of those times in Louisiana when you think that water will never stop coming out of the sky—it was pouring down like God's judgment. Daddy was bringing in a well. The roughnecks had to work in all kinds of weather, of course—oil doesn't wait for good weather. Daddy's special job in the oil field was called "stabbing pipe," which meant he had to be at the top of the oil derrick, 150 feet up, guiding the pipe into the ground. He was there in the summer heat and in the winter sleet storm and in spring when the sky cracked open and dumped sheets of rain day after day. I worried about Daddy all the time, but I especially worried when the weather was bad.

Daddy got in after midnight. He was drunk, water streaming like the fury off his yellow slicker, and he had something in his arms, an animal wrapped in one of his old work shirts.

I could see a black nose poking out one end of the bundle and a stringy tail hanging out the other. The creature was soaked and shivering. What's that, Daddy? I asked.

It's a mama-dog, he said. He swayed as he spoke. Look. He drew the cloth away from the dog's face so that I could see. I saw sheer terror looking back from dark eyes. The little critter was trembling all over.

Why did you bring her home?

Why, Sis, they was being mean to her and kicking her around and mistreating her, 'cause she was pregnant, and all. Poor little thing. Daddy looked down at her as if she were a baby. She's a good dog, though. A sweet dog. Water dripped from his slicker onto the floor. She's going to have her pups soon, he said.

What's that you've got there, James? Big Papa had heard the commotion and had gotten up out of bed to see what was happening. He came into the breakfast room in his long johns, with his cane.

It's a mama-dog. I'm gonna let her stay under the house, 'cause she's pregnant and somebody dumped her. He tried not to slur his words, but he didn't fool Papa.

Papa frowned and pointed his cane at Daddy's feet. James, James—we don't need an animal to take care of. We don't need another mouth to feed. And here you are drinking again. Why do you want to worry us this way?

She won't be any trouble, Daddy said. I'll take care of her. He put the shirt back over her face and started an unsteady walk toward the back door. Sis, get me a cardboard box. We got to make her a bed under the house.

Papa went on back to bed mumbling to himself about how Daddy would be the ruination of the family and how much more could they stand in their old age and so on and so forth.

I brought an old towel and some dry rags, and Daddy and I dried the dog off and put the rags in the box for her to sleep on. I got her a pan of milk, too. She wouldn't drink any milk that night, but by the next day, the pan of milk was empty. The sun was out, and I coaxed Mama-dog out into the yard. She was tan, her thin coat stretched tight over her ribs and belly, swollen as it was with the pups. At first she kept her head down and her thin tail between her legs. She flinched at every movement. But I petted her and petted her and talked sweet to her, and she seemed to lose some of her scare. Finally she turned her head and licked my hand.

Mama-dog had her pups—there were six of them, and Daddy found homes for them all. I kept Mama-dog, though. Jim and Donna played with her, too, but Mama-dog really belonged to me. To me and Daddy.

CHAPTER 6

in which I learn God is a bully

BIG PAPA WAS AN IMPOSING FIGURE, HANDSOME IN HIS YOUTH, STILL WITH a full head of blonde hair, who came out of the Victorian husband-as-God school. Each day he dressed with care, often with a vest and a tie and always with his gold pocket watch. He walked tall and straight, albeit with a cane, up the hill to the courthouse to play dominos with his cronies.

Granny and Big Papa didn't go to church at this point in their lives. Getting dressed and getting there was an obstacle, since Papa didn't drive anymore. Big Papa was a deacon for life, though, and so occasionally the minister would call him up and ask him to come on down to the church and deliver the Sunday morning prayer at the worship service. Papa's church prayer was formal and respectful, similar to his table grace, only it was considerably longer and had no mention of food. God was addressed as if He were a bank president. The prayer always ended, And help us to walk circumspectly with Thee.

I have never heard anyone else use the word "circumspectly," either then or since. Big Papa, I began to see, was scared of God. He thought of God as a Big Bully in the Sky—a highly moral bully, but a bully nevertheless. And with the 18th century chain of being still intact in our household, of course, Papa became our Big Bully. He was fearsome still, though he had lost the physical strength and meanness of spirit that had made him an anathema to his seven children. We did not "talk back." If we disagreed with a decree, we kept it to ourselves. Although he let us know of his disapproval, we knew he would never strike us, as he had done his own children, because Daddy had warned him he had better never touch one of us.

We were good children—quiet, respectful, obedient. We didn't give trouble either at home or at school. Once in a while one of us would get into minor mischief—as when my little sister Donna sharpened her crayons in Big Papa's pencil sharpener. Big Papa lined us up and demanded that we confess who had done the deed. When a confession wasn't forthcoming, he said, You know, we don't have to take you children in. If you can't behave, you can just get out. I never had the feeling that home was a refuge protecting me from the vagaries of the outside world. Actually, it was the outside world – school and church – that gave me some escape from the vagaries of home.

Big Papa lived with burdens that he never spoke of, but which became more pronounced as he grew older. It was whispered that his early retirement as Postmaster was caused by a "nervous condition." I can believe that. For as long as we lived there in Homer, Big Papa thought he had cancer. He did not have cancer—he had guilt. He regularly sent money to an outfit called the Coxey Cancer Clinic, which advertised on the Radio Gospel Bible Hour, beamed in all the way from Del Rio, Texas.

Every evening whoever was at home was expected to join Big Papa around the radio to hear Brother J. Harold Smith, who dealt out quite a quantity of fire and brimstone. Papa was hard of hearing and so we had to turn the volume up high, and even then Papa cupped his hand around his left ear and tilted his head so as to hear better.

For all have sinned and come short of the glory of God, Romans 3:23, J. Harold shouted through the big boxy radio. *All* have sinned, the scripture says, and *all* means you, my brother and you, my sister. Yes, every *one* of you listening out there in radio land tonight. The scripture is talking to you. You may hide your sin from your neighbor. You may hide your sin from your family. You may even hide your sin from the church. But let me tell you one thing, brothers and sisters: you can't hide your sin from God—He knows your heart, and He sees clean *through* you.

J. Harold went on like this for half an hour, until all us listeners were good and guilty, and then he started in on his salvation message: All you have to do is turn your life and your will over to Jesus, and He'll save you. He'll save you tonight. Don't wait, don't wait another minute. You never know what tomorrow will bring. You never know when God's hand will pluck you out of this life and into the next. Will you be ready? Will you? Come on home, come on home tonight, to Jesus. Then the choir began, Softly and tenderly Jesus is calling, calling to you and to me . . .

When he figured everyone was saved who was going to get saved, he began his sales pitch. Send in your donations to support the Radio Gospel Bible Hour, brothers and sisters, and you'll surely be blessed by the Lord. And brothers and sisters, if you send in ten dollars, only the small sum of ten dollars, Brother J. Harold Smith is gonna send you a copy of the King James Version of the *Bible* with the words of Jesus in red! And remember if you have a prayer request, put that in with your check. Keep those cards and letters comin' in, friends, keep 'em comin' in. God bless you, and goodnight.

Big Papa would sometimes snap off the radio to the closing strains of the gospel music, and shake his head again and again, falling into a paroxysm of guilt and self-recrimination. Your sins will catch up with you, he would say. Your sins will find you out. When I was young, I didn't pay the Lord any mind. Havin' a big time was all I thought of—I was wild as a March hare. Now I'm paying the price. Oh Lord, take this burden from me, oh Lord forgive me for my transgressions.

God as moral judge, God as purveyor of punishment: for most of my life, my concept of God was based on my grandfather. Big Papa was the one who set down the rules, who kept the standards, such as they were. He regularly called out Daddy's transgressions, which we children were all too familiar with anyway, and so my father had no moral authority. My grandmother was virtuous, but passive. All the moral strength lay with Big Papa: this frightened, mean-spirited, often selfish man, who dominated the household. No wonder I withheld so much of myself from my God. No wonder I kept my most delicious thoughts hidden.

CHAPTER 7

in which I learn that killing is wrong

MY BROTHER JIM GOT A BB GUN FOR CHRISTMAS ONE YEAR, AND WE couldn't wait to try it out. We put on our heavy jackets and went out back to set up some tin cans on the fence posts separating our yard from the Endom's. The cold was sharp, and our breath came out frosty white as we set up the cans. Then we moved back about fifteen yards through the remains of the garden, over the hard clumps of earth that held dried bean vines and skeletal okra stalks, and took aim, each in turn. Ping! This is easy, I thought. Ping, ping! I took off my gloves to have better control of the trigger.

I caught movement out of the corner of my eye as I made ready for my next shot.

Look—cedar waxwings! said Jim, pointing. A small, scraggly group of the yellow-gray birds had paused for rest in the top of the old china berry tree, whistling and turning their curious heads this way and that. Let's shoot some!

Without so much as a thought, I turned the gun away from the tin cans up toward the tree. I caught one bird in the V-shaped sight and slowly, slowly squeezed the trigger. This time there was no ping as the pellet reached its target, and the little bird fell silently to the ground.

You got one, Sis!

Unbelieving, I raced forward to see what I had done.

I picked up the feathered lump from under the tree and looked at it closely. It was still warm, but it was dead. The head wobbled around and the eyes were staring open and the little feet were curling up. I didn't know I was going to do this, that I *could* do this, that I had this kind of power, to make something alive dead—I mean, ants and mosquitos are one thing but this singing, flying, feathery thing was something else. I wished I could go back and erase the time, change the moment just before I pulled the trigger, do it all over, and this time just aim and pretend to shoot but not really shoot. I didn't mean to kill anything! But I couldn't change what I had done, and there was no way I could make the bird fly again.

Right in the breast—see, right here, you can see where the BB went in, said Jim. Great shot! He started to take the bird from me, to get a closer look himself.

No! I screamed, and whirled away from him, surprised at the fury in my voice. It's my bird, I killed it and it's my bird, you leave it alone.

OK, big deal, so it's your bird, who wants a stupid dead bird, anyway. Why are you so mad? I just want to *see* it, that's all.

I have to bury it.

What?

I have to bury it.

Why?

Because I killed it. Don't you understand? It's dead, and I killed it.

It's only a bird, Sis. Besides, the ground is frozen hard as a rock. You can't even dig in the stupid ground.

Leave me alone! You're the one who's stupid!

Jim turned to pick up the gun from the ground where I had dropped it.

See if you ever use *my* BB gun again, he said. You're just a stupid girl. He shook the gun at me and stalked away.

Jim was right about one thing—the ground was too hard to dig. Even with the hoe I couldn't make much headway, so I found a trench-like place near the fence and put the cedar waxwing in it and then collected rocks and piled them over the bird until I had a mound that the cats in the neighborhood couldn't get into. Then I made a little cross out of two china berry sticks and tied it together with some bark and stuck it in the rock pile. I knew the marker wouldn't stay there long, but it made me feel better.

I was ashamed for months after that whenever I saw a flock of birds flying or hovering together in a tree. I didn't understand myself for wanting to shoot one and knew that I would never kill anything for fun again because I knew it was not fun, it was bad. I knew everyone didn't feel this way, like Mr. Ketcham, who donated all those heads of wild African beasts he shot to the library. I had to see them every time I went there, and I always used to think how they were alive and happy before Mr. Ketcham shot them down just to prove he could do it. How would he like to be stuffed and hanging over the biographies?

CHAPTER 8

in which Daddy almost dies

Where is Daddy? The thought keeps running through my head. He has been gone for four days, with no call, no word. I am always afraid he's dead when he doesn't come home. He and his buddy Ray Chadwick go out just looking for trouble sometimes, and Ray is from a no-count family, Granny says, and besides he is given to drink, so what could you expect but trouble. Daddy won't dodge it if it's coming his way, he'll back Ray up, no matter what, and Ray the same with Daddy.

The other day Papa sat back in his big easy chair, knocked the old tobacco out of his pipe on the metal pipe stand, and said, I wouldn't take a million dollars for one of these grandbabies, and I wouldn't give a nickel for one more just like them, which I suppose was intended to be a compliment but somehow it felt like a slight, to me. I started thinking what life would be like without Daddy.

I wish James would come on home, Granny says, and at that very moment, we hear him at the front door.

Hey, Daddy says, in a drunken voice. I feel myself stop being so scared, *oh, Jesus thank you, Daddy's home!* and at the same time a sick feeling rises inside. *He's drunk again.* I start towards his voice and then hear him fall just inside the front door. I run to him, try to rouse him, try to help him up, but I'm not strong enough.

Go get Jim! Granny says, and I run as fast as I can down to the Endom's house where Jim is shooting BB guns with his best friend Ronnie. Jim, Daddy's sick, come help, come quick! And Jim, who is twelve and a big strong boy, throws down his gun and runs, me following as fast as I can up to the house where Daddy is lying as still as stone, in the same spot where he fell.

I look at Daddy's face, and he looks like an old man he is so pale and sick-looking, and Granny says, hurry, get him to the back bedroom and let him rest, and Jim and I somehow get him back there and he falls like a sack of meal on the bed. We loosen his clothes so he can rest and all the time my heart is thumping out loud because he looks so bad. I never saw Daddy look this sick before, and I begin thinking again what it would be like not to have a daddy at all and just be there with Granny and Papa and Jim and Donna all by myself and no fishing trips and no plum hunting and worst of all, being scared all the time.

We get him in bed, and Granny goes over to take his pulse, because he does look like a dead man. She feels of his wrist and feels of it again, and a third time she feels for his heartbeat, and she pulls back and she says, Your daddy's got no pulse, he's gone, and she drops to her knees on the spot and starts praying out loud to the Lord to save her son James and to forgive him for his drinking and to bring him back to life because he has these three babies to raise, and her hands are in the air, begging God to hear, and Jim and I are both crying because we don't know what to do and Granny's voice is so loud and powerful, I never saw her this way before. Sure enough the Lord hears her, because Daddy starts breathing again, and Granny stays on her knees to give thanks, yes, she does, she gives thanks that her baby son has been delivered once again.

CHAPTER 9

in which my anger frightens me

I WAS CUTTING UP A CHICKEN THE FIRST TIME I HAD THE FANTASY ABOUT cutting Granny. She was standing at the kitchen cabinet making biscuits, with her hands full of the soft, light dough (nobody made biscuits as light as Granny's), and I was about to chop hard through the breastbone with the big iron chopping knife and this picture of Granny came before me and I saw for a moment the knife cutting into the white tender flesh of a Granny and not the chicken breast.

A cold finger ran up my spine: I didn't know where that killing picture came from, but I knew that it must have come from somewhere inside of me, where else, and how could I trust myself, the self underneath the school self, the church-going self, the sweet little girl self, if monsters with knives are there, ready for no reason to appear and hurt an old Granny.

Now this is the best Granny you could want to have, I said to myself—why this woman is pure good all the way through, everyone says so, she raised seven children of her own, plus partly raised six belonging to other people, and had boarders in and fed them, too—she even cut her very hair and made hair braids to sell when money was short. She worked all the time, all the time, for her family—why there wasn't a selfish bone in her body, that's what everybody said about Granny.

Granny is standing naked at the washbasin in the bathroom, wiping her sweating body with a washcloth on which she has put a little Ivory soap. The soap smell and the sweet smell of perspiration are heavy in the steaming air and I, eleven years of age, feel quivery in my stomach. I am helping Granny so that she will not fall in the bathroom. Granny washes her face and her neck, then her breasts, flat empty against her body, then underarms, her dimpled-through wrinkled flesh hanging down soft from the bone, and then she widens her legs and bends slowly and washes between her legs and the sweet old woman smell is stronger and a few gray hairs cling to her private parts, the lips, flaps hang soft, useless from her body.

I turn away and look at the tall white cabinet behind Granny where all the medicines are kept, and I see old prescription drugs alongside of rusty cans empty of Band-Aids, and bottles of Watkins Liniment, and Geritol, and old jars of Vaseline, and two filthy combs, and cold tablets and on and on and on and I feel sick and Granny says, I'm almost through, Hon, in her soft, sweet voice and I hold on for a few minutes longer. I help Granny slip her old blue nightgown over her head. Steam fills the air. I breathe all this in.

I walk Granny down the hall to bed. Will you pray with me, Marilyn Jane? she asks and I say all right and I crawl into Granny's double bed with her and listen, and Granny prays for all her children, each one by name: Bernadine and Ernie and Varnel and Eugene and Mellie and Lemos and finally James, my daddy who everybody calls "Jim" except his mother, and she prays about James's drinking in roadhouses and prays for his safety at work on the oilrig and prays that the Lord will lead him to a better way. Then she prays for friends and neighbors in need and she prays for the President of the United States and then to finish off her prayers, she prays for all for whom it is our duty to pray, the world over. And she says to me—though in truth I nodded off during the President's prayer— she says, Marilyn Jane, say the Lord's Prayer, Honey, and I do, and I kiss Granny, who has the softest and sweetest flesh in the world, and I say, Goodnight, Granny, I love you.

Goodnight, Honey, Granny says, and turns to sleep.

❧

I didn't tell anybody about my bad thoughts around cutting Granny, because who could I tell, and anyway I thought maybe I was going a little crazy, because I never knew of any sane person wanting to hurt their old grandmother. So I just made sure the knives were in the drawer where they were supposed to be, and when these bad thoughts came, I tried to put them out of my mind, and I tried not to be using knives when Granny was in the kitchen. Not that I would ever hurt my Granny, I knew I wouldn't. It was almost like in church where I sometimes felt an urge to scream a bad word during the most sacred time, but I knew I wouldn't ever. I didn't like thinking about hurting Granny, though. It was a puzzlement to me, and I hoped I would outgrow it, which I did after a year or two. I got to where I could cut up a chicken—WHAP!—and not think of Granny at all.

CHAPTER 10

in which I am in awe of my father

I REMEMBER THE DAY OF THE SWAN DIVE. THE HEAT WAS HOVERING around 100 degrees, and had been for two days running. It was so hot that nobody felt like doing anything but drinking iced tea and fanning themselves out on the front porch and even fanning didn't do that much good, because you ended up fanning hot air right back in your face.

Granny had the hose out front, watering the thick carpet of St. Augustine grass. Papa was sitting in his big rocker on the porch in his thin-string undershirt, waving off flies and wiping his wet fore-head with a big white handkerchief, and reading Zane Grey. Granny had on her gray voile dress, one that used to be a dress-up dress, but was beyond church now, and beyond repair. It was almost as thin as the air itself and fluttered easily in the breeze when there was a breeze, which there wasn't that day.

Daddy was off work, and restless, as he often was after the crew brought in a well. He was sitting with no shirt at all in the other big rocker on the front porch, smoking a Picayune and reading *True Detective*, sweating just like Papa. I asked him if he would take us swimming, and then he surprised me—he said, OK, Sis. I might even go myself. That water would feel good.

Daddy had never, ever been swimming with us, so I couldn't imagine that he was serious. But he went into the back bedroom and came out with a towel and an ancient-looking swimsuit. It had never occurred to me that he might own a swimsuit.

Donna and Jim and I climbed into the big blue-green Olds 88 with Daddy and took off for the city pool. Daddy always had a good car because he drove long distances to oil fields around Louisiana and East Texas, drove on all kinds of roads, and that car had to carry four or five roughnecks and their oil-soaked clothes, plus tin hats and lunch boxes. Twenty years later when I became an impoverished single mother, I sold my Volvo and bought an ancient Oldsmobile—blue-green, of course—with fins and a few dents, cheap. That car would take no prisoners, and I felt safe in it. Reminded me of Daddy, reminded me of home.

On the way to the pool Daddy talked about how he used to swim all the time—in fact, he said what he and Mother did when they first met in Washington, D.C., in the thirties, was to go swimming just about every day after work. And he could dive, too, he said. He learned that in high school.

Now I had never seen my daddy in water, but I had seen his football pictures and his basketball and baseball pictures, and had heard all his stories many times, and so I knew that he was a fine athlete. He never finished high school because he made the varsity football team in the eighth grade, and the rule was that students could play only four years, so why stay in school, he figured.

Daddy would say from time to time, generally when he was drinking, Have you kids ever seen my football picture? Of course, we had seen it dozens of times. But we would say, no, let's see it, and he would go to the back bedroom and take it out of its safe place and show it to us once again. His eyes would begin to redden as he talked, and then the silent tears would come. Coach Wilbanks, he was my coach, and he loved me. He called me Rural Route, because Papa was postmaster. He used to say, Rural Route, win one for me.

And we kids would look at the picture again.

Daddy played center. He wasn't all that big, compared to the other players, and centers take a lot of punishment, he said, since their job is to protect the quarterback. They get hit over and over again, just about every play. Daddy said he could take it, could take anything they could hand out. He was tough, he said. In his junior year they played the Jesuits out of New Orleans. There were no divisions in those days, no class AA and B—everybody played everybody else. And Homer won the state championship. He would pause and look at the picture again, would remember the team and the coach with the graying hair parted down the middle and the black and white striped shirt, smiling broadly.

Coach Wilbanks. I loved that man. I would do anything for him.

There was not a lot to do in Homer. The swimming pool was the pride of the community. It was a grand, Olympic-size pool, complete with a slide at the shallow end, and two baby pools, one for preschoolers and one for kids even smaller. And of course there was the deep end, where the good swimmers stayed, and where the four diving boards were.

Daddy parked on the hill just above the pool, and as I got out, I remember seeing the whole expanse of the water, green and glittering in the sun, filled with bouncing figures. *Daddy was going swimming!*

I came out of the dressing room, jumped in the pool, and looked for Daddy. I saw him swimming in the deep end, stroking and breathing in rhythm, doing what I would later find out was the Australian crawl. Back and forth he went across the pool, looking as if the water were his natural home, making hardly a ripple as he swam. A muscular arm rose gently out of the water with each stroke, and the tips of his fingers reached out to the water, reached out again and again, touching and moving. It was somehow thrilling to me, seeing my daddy move like a great fish in the water.

He stopped at the side of the pool to rest and looked for me. I raised myself waist-high out of the water and waved my hand high in the air, hoping he would see me. He did, and pointed then to the diving board. I caught my breath. He was going to try it!

I watched my father climb the diving boards. He passed the first level, as I thought he would. But he also passed the second-level board and the third level, and much to my surprise, went on up to the top board. Hardly anyone ever dove off the top board. Maybe he would make a fool of himself and land in a pancake. Or maybe he would hurt himself and never rise up out of the water.

He went out to the end of the board and bounced up and down a few times, trying the spring, and then repeated the movement, exquisitely balanced. His form was perfect there in the sun, and I thought that no man could ever be so beautiful as my father on that summer day.

Never taking my eyes from his figure, I held my breath and tightened my body, wanting to help him. He made his approach slowly, as if in a dream, or in slow motion: one step, two steps, both feet on the tip of the board—and then he sprang high into the air, with his arms outstretched, like a magnificent bird. He became a part of the very air into which his body floated. He was a white crane, wild, with wings floating on the air, weightless. And as he turned his head downward towards the depths of the water, the lower half of his body rose up to the sky, and his hands touched together. Down, down, down he came. He entered the water with scarcely a splash, clean as a hot knife into butter.

Awestruck, I watched as Daddy emerged from the water and swam slowly to the side of the pool. How could my father be what I had not known him to be? What other powers would I discover, what else remained unknown?

CHAPTER 11

in which I come of age

IT WAS NOT EVEN LIGHT YET WHEN DADDY CAME INTO MY ROOM, SHAKING my shoulder, trying to get me up. Come on, Hon, wake up. Wake up, those fish will be biting at sunup. We got to get outta here.

I dragged myself out of a dream, pushed back the quilts, and made my way through the dark to the chair where I had left my jeans and flannel shirt the night before, and fumbled them on. I was beginning to wake up, but not ready as yet for light. We would eat breakfast on the road, Daddy said. This was a special day—just Daddy and I were going. Just the two of us. I was old enough to row the boat now, Daddy had said.

As I went out the front door, I saw that Daddy had the big Olds all ready to go. The trunk was open, and I could make out his tackle box, a small net for the shiners, and a bigger one for the bream or bass we were expecting to catch. And Daddy's fly rod, of course. There was a cardboard box full of food: saltines, Vienna sausage, sardines, apples and oranges. He had even boiled some eggs. Our cane poles were resting on the floorboard of the front seat and sticking out through the back window. I watched him. *He is handsome. He's so good-looking.*

Daddy started up the car and got the heater humming, then rolled out so that I could slide in from the driver's side and take my place in the front seat beside him. We were off!

Driving through the night with Daddy was an adventure. Who knew what might lie ahead? Daddy said we were going to the

36

Nigger Camp on Lake Bistineau. It was the best camp on the whole lake for catching bream, he said, because an old nigra woman fed the fish at certain secret spots, and they were sure to be biting there. She had already promised to teach me how to catch bream with a cane pole.

We stopped once on the way, for breakfast, just like Daddy promised, at the truck stop. There was a big neon sign **EAT**, with an arrow underneath, and a smaller hand-painted sign that said

Bread
Milk
Worms

Hi, Jimmy, how're you, Hon? said the waitress, her eyes lighting up when she saw Daddy. Her copper-colored hair was growing out dark at the roots. Smiling and wiping her hands on her white apron, she reached for menus.

Hey, what you got good this mornin', Flora?

I don't reckon much has changed since you were here last, she answered, putting a menu and a steaming cup of coffee in front of each of us.

No, thank you, Ma'am, I don't drink coffee yet, I said, surprised. No one had ever offered me coffee.

Flora, this is my daughter Marilyn. She's my oldest. Didn't I show you her picture before? We're going down to the Nigger Camp.

Well, she's a pretty one. How're you, Hon? I managed a little smile and then retreated to my menu.

Daddy and I both had the same thing: two eggs over easy, curly bacon, grits swimming in butter, big fluffy buttermilk biscuits, and strawberry jam. I ate 'til I thought I would never want to see food again.

We got to the camp just about at sunup. The new sun was shining through trees draped with Spanish moss, reaching their black trunks out of the lake. Long-necked water birds were winging it from branch to branch, resting for a moment and calling out their good-morning sounds before moving on to search the water. The mosquitoes were still thick, and I kept slapping at them as we walked towards the camp. The building itself was really nothing more than a shack made out of weathered gray boards. But inside we were able to rent a boat and buy the bait we needed. We got shiners, catalpa worms, and red wigglers.

Old Elmira, the black woman who was going to teach me to catch bream was outside, busy putting hooks, weights, and corks on a bunch of cane poles. She was a tiny woman, dressed in an old cotton dress, a coarse feed-sack print. A wide-brimmed straw hat covered her grizzled hair. She agreed to take me out as soon as she finished rigging the poles.

They be jumpin' awright this mornin', Miss Marilyn. I been hearin' 'em. You an' me, we goin' to catch a mess. I bets we gets more fish than Mr. James. You come wif me, Chile.

And so I did. Daddy went off in his boat to fly-fish. We were to meet back at the camp at noon.

Old Elmira was as good as her word. She eased our rowboat through the water with hardly a sound, never once bumping one of the many stumps or fallen logs sticking up out of the water. We soon rounded a bend and pulled into what looked to be a small, protected cove. The wind didn't ripple the water there, and there was no debris to prevent us from quietly pulling in.

You wan a catalpa or a wiggler? asked Elmira. I had seen Daddy use catalpas before, and I just couldn't bear the thought of touching those big yellow caterpillars, much less stringing them on a hook and watching them squirt out their yellow juice.

A wiggler, please, I replied.

I watched as Elmira demonstrated how to bait a hook. Them fish is smart, make no bones about it, she said. So we got to out-smart Mr. Fish. You sticks your hook once in this fellah, and throw him in, and you jest feedin' them fish. They'll have him gone in no time. And she showed me how to grasp my worm at one end, between my thumb and forefinger, and then string the whole squirming length of him onto the hook.

Now you try it, Miss Marilyn.

I hated the thought of it, but went ahead anyway. After several tries, I got my hook in one end and then, more or less, got the rest of the worm strung on. He was wiggling frantically, and that nasty, sweet worm smell rose in the air.

Yuck, I said, reaching my hand over the side to rinse the worm juice off. Now what?

Elmira showed me how to set my cork for the right depth, and then how to toss the line with one whipping motion of the cane pole. Now you jes watch your cork, Miss Marilyn. Ever once in a while you bobble it like this, jus to catch them fish's attention, she said, as she raised and lowered her cork just a bit, several times in a row. They'll play with you and nibble, nibble, nibble, but when you got one, your cork'll go under, and that's when you snatch, straight up.

And then she showed me where the best spot was to put my line. No sooner than I dropped it in, a big bream jumped on it. I jerked up and out he came, flapping his blue sides in the morning sun. Again and again, I baited my hook, and hardly ever lost a worm. I soon forgot about the suffering of the worms and the nasty worm smell. Catching fish was all that mattered. Elmira showed me how to slide my hand back over the head and hold the fins down to take the hook out. The big ones we strung on a line, and the small ones we threw back in.

No need to keep them babies, said Elmira. They not ready yet. We be back for them next year.

We returned a little before noon, me triumphant, with two lines of big bream. Daddy was already back and had had less luck: two little bass. His face had gotten some sun. They're not biting worth a damn, he said. As soon as the sun got up, they wouldn't strike at all. He shook his head and reached into his pocket for a cigarette.

Well, let's have some lunch and we'll go back when it cools off some. Marilyn, this time I'll show you how to row, and then I can concentrate on the fishing.

Late that afternoon we set out once again. With the waning of the light, the water grew darker and took on new depths. The tree trunks grew blacker, and the Spanish moss lacier and more luxuriant against the rosy hues of the sky. As we moved out into the lake, we seemed to be entering magical space.

Then I saw the snake. It was a long black fellow swimming through the water just about four feet from our boat. At one point he stopped swimming and stuck his head about four inches out of the water, turning it back and forth and flicking his tongue as if in question. Then he moved on. But he was not the only one. I saw dozens as the evening went on—some swam close enough for me to reach out and touch, had I dared to. Others draped themselves lazily in the moss-covered branches of trees under which Daddy rowed. I was terrified that one would drop into the boat, but Daddy told me not to worry, that that was not likely to happen, and if it did, he could take care of the situation. I trusted him in this, as I trusted him in all things, and finally accepted the snakes as a given.

Try as I might, I could not master rowing. Whenever we came to a spot where the fish were biting, I ended up paddling the boat directly over that spot and then turning it in circles, scaring all the fish away as I tried to maneuver. Daddy finally took over the rowing, and both of us fished. I caught a few more bream, and finally, near sunset, Daddy snagged a good-sized bass.

It was dark when our boat slipped into shore, taking its place among the others. Only the lights of the camp allowed us to see at all. Daddy began cleaning the fish to fry for supper, and I waded barefoot along the edge of the lake, my feet luxuriating in the mud and warm water. I noticed a broad board leading further into the dark water and decided to walk the length of it. Balancing myself with both arms out, I suddenly slid down the muddy board, jamming a nail between the big and second toes of my right foot. I shrieked, and Daddy came running. There I was, still upright, nailed to that muddy board.

Daddy pulled my foot back from the nail, then examined the wound. It went deep. And the nail was a rusty one. He decided that we had to go into the nearest town and get me a tetanus shot. No telling when was the last time I had had one.

When we arrived at the emergency room, we were ushered right in—nothing going on in the sleepy little town that night. The clerk was taking down all the information.

The patient's name then is Marilyn Jane Fulmer? She is your wife, Mr. Fulmer?

No, my daughter, Daddy said. I blushed. *Why would anyone think that I was married to Daddy? Can't she see that I'm only twelve? Just like at the truck stop when the waitress tried to give me coffee.* All the same, after I had my tetanus shot and we walked out, I did feel somehow older. Daddy guided me along as I had seen men guide women, by touching an elbow.

That night we stayed in a cabin, the only one at the camp. It was off in the forest, down a winding trail, a good distance from the main building. It was built of the same weathered gray wood as the camp house. As I entered the screen door, the light from a single kerosene lamp revealed the simple furnishings—a small rickety table, a couple of wooden chairs, and a bed. One bed. *Where was I to sleep?*

Looks like you'll have to sleep with me, Hon, said Daddy. There's just the one bed.

Daddy slept in his shorts, as he always did. I had often seen his body flung out in rest in the back bedroom, trying to stay cool enough to sleep after returning from work on the oilrig. Sometimes the placket in his shorts would fall open, and I would glimpse his male parts, soft and mysterious.

Daddy turned his back to me and began to doze. I quickly put on my gown and slipped into the bed beside him. I felt strange. I shouldn't be sleeping with Daddy, I knew. I was too old. Hadn't

Granny said I was "filling out" and shouldn't undress in front of Jim or Big Papa anymore?

He went to sleep right away, but I couldn't. The soft mattress made the bed sink down on his side, so that every time I let myself relax, I rolled over beside him, his weight was so much more than mine. I stayed awake for what seemed like hours until fatigue finally overcame me, and I gave myself to my dreams.

The next thing I knew, Daddy was shaking me and saying, Marilyn, Honey, it's only a dream. But I wouldn't stop moaning, and so he held me and stroked my face and my hair. Hush, Sweetheart, it's only a dream. Daddy's here. Daddy's here. I finally quieted back into sleep.

The next morning's fishing was disappointing, so we packed up and made ready to go. On our way out, we stopped by the Camp to tell Elmira goodbye.

Bye, Miss Marilyn, Elmira said, smiling up from her fishing poles. You and Mr. James come again real soon. She sho is a nice chile, Mr. James.

CHAPTER 12

in which I save Ida

BLACK WOMEN HELPED RAISE US, AS THEY DID MOST OF THE WHITE CHILdren growing up in the South. First there was Christine, later Ida and Marguerite.

Christine was with us the longest. She was a large woman, bigboned and solid. Solid like a granite boulder, or perhaps an ancient tree. She moved silently through the house, cleaning, cooking, washing, ironing. I felt quiet inside when she was near. At some point, Christine got a job that paid two dollars a week more, and so she moved on. I thought about her after she was gone, and I wanted her back. But I didn't see her again until my grandmother's funeral, many years later. The church was crowded, the service I really don't remember. But I do remember looking up in the balcony just before the service and seeing one lone figure, a large black woman with graying hair. Christine had come to pay her last respects.

Marguerite was the only person who saw that I was turning into a woman. Miss Marilyn, you sho is lookin' tall an' pretty these days, she said one day, talking over her shoulder as she hung out white sheets on the line. You gonna be a right pretty woman, you are. I blushed. How could I ever be pretty, with my thick glasses and broken-out skin? But Marguerite said so. And Marguerite was right about most things.

Ida believed in ghosts—or so she said. We children used to listen to her tell ghost stories as she stirred the cornbread or made pastry for the fried apple pies, punctuating her words with periodic slaps on the bread board, causing a little cloud of flour to rise each time she turned over the round pieces of dough with her black hands.

An then that ole ghostes said, "I'm gwina git you, yeah, I am," and the next day, that ole wicked farmer was found out in the punkin patch, dead, wif his eyes plucked out, and his heart sittin' besides him in the field. Ida would pause, her eyes growing big.

It's God's truth, it happen jes that way. It don't pay to do no bad things, l'il chillun. Cause ifen you do, the ghostes will getcha. Boo! We would jump, and squeal with laughter. Now, get out from under foot so's I can finish these pies.

One afternoon when I was about eleven, I was out on the front porch playing with Mama Dog when I heard Big Papa roaring at someone in the back of the house. I yanked open the screen door and ran inside to see what was happening. When I got to the breakfast room, I saw that Big Papa had his fist up in the air, as if he were about to hit Ida. His face was red and twisted and he was yelling, You're a thief, a thief, I knew it!

No, Mister Fuller, I didn't steal nothin', said Ida.

Don't talk back to me, nigger, Papa screamed. I'll knock your head off! He raised his fist again. Ida drew back, cringing and shielding her head with one arm. Two fried apple pies had fallen to the floor, where they lay cracked open, oozing their warm sweet juice.

Miz Fulmer, she give me them pies, said I could have one for me and one for each of my chillun. I been workin' fo' you fo' goin' on six years now, Mr. Fulmer. I ain't never taken nothin' from you.

I said don't talk back to me! Papa's eyes looked red, like some devil's.

I was shaking. First my fingers, then my hands, then my arms. My bones seemed to be coming loose from their moorings. NO-O-O-O! I screamed from somewhere in the very depths of myself. I had never before dared to raise my voice to Big Papa, and I was surprised at these sounds coming from within.

Big Papa put down his fist and stared at me. For about ten seconds I shook uncontrollably, then my body seemed to quiet. I looked directly at him, and I said, Those are *Ida's* pies. Granny gave them to her.

Big Papa never apologized to Ida at all, he just said, Huh! and whirled around and stalked out of the breakfast room. I looked at Ida, who was standing like stone, with one hand over her mouth, her eyes white with fear.

That is the image I am left with. When I imagine the aftermath, I see the two of us bending to the floor and beginning to clean up the ruined pies, my small white hand and Ida's big calloused hand, together, picking up the pieces, wiping the surface clean again. But I don't know that the scene played out that way. I want to believe I had the presence of mind and the goodness of heart, even as a child, to join Ida in some redemptive act. I doubt that I did.

CHAPTER 13

in which I leave the Catholic Church

MY MOTHER WAS A DEVOUT CATHOLIC WHO ATTENDED MASS EACH morning. When she married my father, she made him promise that their children would be raised Catholic, and so my religious beginnings were steeped in that tradition. She was a young woman when we left her—in her late thirties, she would have been—but she never remarried or even dated anyone. She said, I never looked at another man after your father. Once you were married, you were married for life, she believed. But I think her lack of interest in men was grounded in something far deeper even than her religious faith. She never stopped loving Daddy.

She gave her last good years as a cook for a houseful of priests. God was an abiding presence for her when situations went awry, which they almost always did, for she was a true romantic. She loved musicals, loved the lights of the city. She was one to gaze at the stars.

As a little Catholic girl living in Cincinnati, I memorized my Catechism, knew the Apostles Creed: "I believe in God the Father Almighty, Maker of heaven and earth. And in Jesus Christ, his only Son . . ." I made my First Communion and was confirmed. We three children went to Holy Name School and were taught by nuns. I noted that these women wore special black, flowing costumes and were respected by everyone, and I wondered briefly if I should become a nun. Was this the way to God?

After we were taken to Louisiana, I walked my little brother and sister to St. Margaret's, the only Catholic church in Homer, every Sunday morning, out of respect for Mother's wishes. But Jim and Donna were reluctant worshippers in what was still a Latin Mass, and they began disturbing services. No matter—I myself soon began having some doubts about the Catholic Church.

One of my main problems with Catholicism was the concept of transubstantiation—the belief that the bread and wine turn into the body and blood of Jesus after the priest blesses them. I asked Father Goubeaux, the priest at St. Margaret's, to explain this: You mean, the wafer really, actually becomes flesh? I mean, inside my stomach, it does? He assured me that it did. I imagined someone taking communion and then being operated on, to see if in fact the wafer had turned to flesh. Try as I would, I simply could not believe that this physical change was possible. My doubts frightened me. I wanted to believe, but I couldn't.

The other practice that bothered me was confession. There were so many sins to be aware of. And not only were there real sins, but if you thought something was a sin and it wasn't, just your thinking that it was, made it a sin. If you neglected to mention even a venial sin when you went to confession, you were then guilty of a mortal sin and in danger of hellfire. My biggest problem was that I felt that some of my sins were in bad taste and therefore unrepeatable. There are some things you just don't tell anyone else. Well, God, maybe. But not the priest. I stopped attending the Catholic church when I was twelve.

Father Goubeaux noticed our absence, and asked my grandmother if he could come for a visit. He was ushered into the living room, where he and I were left alone, to speak in private. The priest sat on one end of the sofa and I on the other. His silver hair stood out like little wings from the sides of his head, and his teeth, which never all quite fit into his mouth, seemed even more prominent than usual. His black cassock carried the whole weight of the Church. Wasting no words, he began: Marilyn Jane, you must come back to St. Margaret's.

But, Father, I don't believe anymore, I said. I can't help it. My fingernails dug into my clasped palms. I tried to explain about communion, but he would have none of it.

Who are you to think that you know more than the Church? The Church is the way to God, Marilyn Jane, and the only way. If the Church tells you that the communion wafer is the flesh of Christ, then that is what it is. You are only a child. It is your place to learn, not to question. He leaned forward, measuring each word – his eyebrows seemed to grow darker and to knit together between his eyes. As he spoke, I noticed specks of white spittle on his lips: You must come back to the Catholic Church, Marilyn Jane, he said. Unless you return, you will burn in hell for all of eternity.

Long seconds passed, and I considered what he said. Then I spoke. Father, do you believe that God knows everything?

Yes, of course, my child. The eyebrows began to relax.

Then it will do me no good to pretend to believe, will it? Because God knows what is really inside me. I can't come back to St. Margaret's because if I do, it'll be like telling a lie to God. I'm sorry you're upset and Mother will be upset when she hears. But how can I tell a lie to God?

That's the problem with God. You can lie to your grandmother, you can lie to the priest, but there's no way to lie to God. You're stuck with the truth.

🐝

CHAPTER 14

in which I am saved

MY GRANDPARENTS DIDN'T MIND WHICH CHURCH I ATTENDED, BUT AFTER I left the Catholics, Big Papa made it clear that I must attend church somewhere. So I decided on their church, which was Southern Baptist. You don't join the Baptist church by just signing a book, as you do with the Unitarian Universalists, or by being sprinkled, as with the Methodists. My Catholic baptism and confirmation didn't count, of course. No, the Baptists insisted that you be baptized like Jesus and John, fully immersed, in order to have all of your sins washed away.

All of my Baptist schoolmates had already been "saved" by the time they were twelve, and so my own salvation was long overdue. Every time the congregation sang the invitation hymn at the end of the church service, asking lost people to come down the aisle and give their lives to Jesus, I felt a good deal of pressure to do just that. Finally, I was pushed over the line one evening by a visiting evangelist named Angel Martinez.

Are you washed in the blood,
In the soul-cleansing blood of the Lamb?
Are your garments spotless,
Are they white as snow,
Are you washed in the blood of the Lamb?

The revival at the First Baptist Church was winding to a close, with Angel preaching. That evening he was wearing his usual out-fit—a white suit and a pastel tie—which set off his dark good looks. He used to be a Catholic, people said, but converted to the Southern Baptist faith.

I kept very still, watching him cut his hand through the air to emphasize a point, compelling people with his fierce dark eyes to heed his words.

Don't you *know* that Jesus loves you? Don't you *know* that he hung on the cross because of your sins? That's right—yours and mine. We put him there. Don't you *know* that he wants you right now, tonight, to say "no" to sin and say "yes" to him? Won't you do it now? Won't you just step out of your seat and come forward?

I stared at him, in awe. He was the most handsome man I had ever seen.

I felt that Angel was looking directly at me. This was the last night of the revival, and I knew my time had come to walk the aisle and be saved. The trouble was that I didn't feel much like a sinner. I knew I was not perfect, but I tried to be good. And then there was this thing about Jesus paying the price. I was clear that I was responsible for whatever sins I did commit and that nobody else could get me off the hook, not even Jesus.

"Softly and tenderly Jesus is calling, calling for you and for me." As the choir sang these familiar words over and over again, pleading for lost sinners to come forward, I felt invisible arms pulling at me. Angel Martinez had come down from the pulpit. He was holding the microphone on a long cord in one hand, his other hand raised high into the air.

Don't wait another minute! Say "yes" to Jesus tonight! Won't you come on now, as the choir sings, come on down the aisle.

My sweaty hands tightened on the hymnal. It was as if the whole congregation was singing to me alone: "Come home, come home, Ye who are weary, come home. Earnestly, tenderly, Jesus is calling, calling, O sinner, come home."

I was praying, as I did each night, that I would be able to find

"God's will" for my life. That prayer was the scariest, the most dangerous to pray. I knew I might be called to go to Africa as a missionary, to save the heathen, and end up dying of some strange disease whose name I couldn't even pronounce. Nevertheless, the time had come.

My feet moved almost without my bidding out into the aisle, and I found myself walking down to the front of the church, where the regular minister, Brother Skelton, was waiting to receive sinners. Angel kept on preaching, ever more urgently. He wiped the perspiration off his forehead with a large white handkerchief. He twisted, he pointed, his dark eyes searched the room. He kept asking people to come on down the aisle.

Bless you, Sister, bless you. Yes, the Holy Spirit is working here tonight! Jesus is calling! Won't you answer Him now? Don't wait until it's too late. The congregation continued to sing, pleading, "Jesus is tenderly calling today . . . "

As Brother Skelton clasped my hand and bent forward to hear, I whispered I want to join the church.

I felt like a very small boat in a very large sea. My insides were churning.

Do you believe that Jesus is your savior?

Yes, sort of, I said, choking on my words.

What's that? he asked, cupping his hand over his ear and leaning closer. I could see his beady black eyes behind his thick glasses.

Yes, I said, feeling more than a little guilty. I didn't really understand what it meant for Jesus to save me, in spite of having heard two sermons on Sunday and one at Wednesday night prayer meeting, for over two years. But I liked what I knew of Jesus. Jesus would, I thought, understand that I was as saved as I could be, at the moment.

The following Sunday night I was baptized, along with the others who were saved during the revival. Most were children younger than myself. We all waited in line in our long white gowns.

When my turn came, Brother Skelton lifted his chin and looked at me and stretched out one arm to help me into the baptismal fount. Without my glasses, I could hardly see where I was going. I moved tentatively down the steps and into the water, struggling to stay upright, the long white robe dragging me down. I swooshed forward and took the preacher's hand.

Marilyn Jane has come asking to be baptized and asking for membership in this church, he declared. We rejoice in her decision to follow Jesus.

As I stood there looking down, my hands folded like some wet, awkward angel, Brother Skelton put one hand on my head and lifted his other hand in the air. Then he whispered in my ear, Don't be afraid. You won't fall.

Marilyn Jane Fulmer, my sister, because of your profession of faith in Jesus Christ as your Lord and savior, I now baptize you . . .

Stiff and uncertain, but held by the preacher's arm, I let myself lean backwards and go under the water and then be raised to my feet once more.

In the name of the Father and the Son and the Holy Spirit. Dead to sin and raised to walk in newness of life. Amen.

The robe had become transparent and was sticking to my skin. I thought probably everybody in church could see my underwear. Water was dripping from my hair and running into my eyes. Feeling naked and half blind, I sloshed out of the fount.

People are supposed to feel different after they are baptized: "Raised to walk in newness of life." I didn't feel new, though. I was still the same person, still sad, still feeling lost. But at least now I was not different from my friends. And now I didn't have to feel so guilty every time the invitation is given at the end of the church service.

I went to church every time the doors opened: Sunday school and church on Sunday morning, choir practice and prayer meeting on Wednesday night, and on Sunday night, Baptist Training Union and the evening worship service. The church was safe and predictable. After the service we had Youth Fellowship at someone's house, where we teenagers formed a prayer circle, said sentence prayers, and sang songs like "How Great Thou Art" and "Kum Ba Yah." I belonged. When we sang "This Little Light of Mine," I came to believe that I had some light to share, and that I would surely find a way to share it someday.

CHAPTER 15

in which I am held in community

MISS ALTALENE WAS A FIXTURE IN THE FABRIC DEPARTMENT AT WHITE'S Dry Goods. She must have been in her seventies by the time I was in high school, but in all the years I knew her, she always looked the same: the short white hair swept back from her face like a starched collar, the large flesh-colored mole just to the left of her mouth, the watery blue eyes, the old-lady glasses and the black pumps with the fat heels. The only thing that changed was the color of her flowered dresses.

Miss Altalene was always smiling, but I couldn't understand why, because she was what we called an old maid. Maybe she had had a suitor once, but gave him up to take care of her parents, I don't know, but there was no one for Miss Altalene. She lived alone.

Well, hello, Marilyn Jane, she says when I enter the store, just like I am the most special person in the world. What can I help you with today? Being near Miss Altalene is like waking up cozy in your bed on Saturday morning with nothing to do. She has that way about her in Sunday school, too, where she is my teacher this year.

I ask her to help me pick out some material for the skirt I am going to make in my Home Economics class. Together we move into the sea of fabric, unrolling the bright bolts and feeling the texture of each, Miss Altalene stroking the cloth with her hand as she talks. Finally, the right one appears, a red wool, rich looking, the color of blood. This is it, this is the one I want! I tell her.

Miss Altalene's smile broadens. Shall I cut it for you then? And she cuts the fabric with sure, careful strokes, and then folds it up into a soft red square for me. I'm imagining that I will look fetching in this beautiful new skirt. Do you need some thread? she asks. And we go over to the bank of colored spools and she helps me find the best match among the reds. We pick out a seven-inch zipper and some hem tape. She adds it all up on a piece of paper, with a stubby pencil. That'll come to $5.59, she says, and I say, Charge it to my daddy. And she does.

Miss Altalene was one of the many people in the church who watched over me. There was Brother Skelton, the minister at First Baptist, veering toward blind, with his coke-bottle glasses. His sermons were quieter, less bombastic than Brother Barker's, the previous minister, but both men knew us Fulmer kids and cared about us. To this day, I miss the singing. So many of the old hymns are in my blood: "The Old Rugged Cross," "Precious Lord, Take My Hand," and of course, "Amazing Grace." I still remember most of the verses. Sometimes when my sister and I get together, we sing the hymns and other church songs like "It Took a Miracle." She's soprano, and I'm alto, just like then.

Miss St. Clair was the children's and youth music director at the church. She was a tall woman, big-boned and stately, with blonde hair that was graying fast, which she wore in a bun on her head. Miss St. Clair had a way of standing close and looking right through you with her large, unblinking green eyes when she spoke to you in a very quiet voice, enunciating every syllable. She would eventually surprise everyone by marrying late, in her forties. She married short, round Mr. Harris after his wife died, though she towered over him. Her smile broadened and came more often, after that.

I had various Sunday School teachers through the years. I got into it once with Winnifred Douglas, because I asked why did Jesus turn the water into wine at the wedding, if drinking is bad, and she said that he didn't turn it into wine, he turned it into grape juice. That didn't sound right to me, but I let it pass. I didn't mind that she was ignorant of certain details in the Scripture—what did it matter, really. What mattered is that she loved me—she loved me, and she showed up without fail every Sunday morning to be there for me and the other members of the Sunday school class.

No one in my family was ever present at church or school events—my varsity basketball games, the football games where I was in the marching band, not even for high school graduation. I didn't think their absence unusual or neglectful—I knew their lives didn't allow such. But when an adult did show up for me, an adult who was constant and caring, I didn't take that lightly. I took no kindness for granted. I still don't.

So even though the theology of the church never quite made sense to me, the church held me. I mattered to the ministers and lay members. I learned about leadership there, I learned to sing, and I learned to pray from my heart. I'll always be grateful.

The church was there, yes, and the neighbors were there—not one of the families on our street moved away while I was growing up. Bob and Irene Thompson lived next door. Bob must have been retired, because he just sat in the swing on his front porch every day. The Gerhardt sisters lived across the street from Bob and Irene. They wore their long hair braided and up on their head, and hardly ever came out. Their house smelled musty. I don't know where they got money to live on.

Mamie and Mike Endom lived down the street on the other side of us with their two sons, Charles and Ronnie. Ronnie was my brother's best friend and his hunting companion. Mike was a railroad man who came home each day to his newspaper and his cigar. He didn't have much to say, but always looked up from his paper and his circle of smoke to greet me with a wide grin when I happened in. Mamie had a temper, and more than once, I saw her chasing her older son Charles with a broom. You come back here! I said come back here! she would yell. Sometimes one of us children would drop in on Mamie around dinnertime, and she would always set us a place. There was an extra glass of iced tea, often some beans from the garden, and a piece of corn bread, hot from the skillet. And she gave us pecans from the huge tree in their yard. I knew all the neighbors on the street—the Whites, a quiet elderly couple; the Boyds, Janis was in my class and her brother Billy was on the football team; Coach Gil, whose little boy looked just like his dad, with that long face and whitish blond hair; the Lays, whose son Dean and I played doctor.

And then there was Leira Chrisler.

CHAPTER 16

in which I question God's plan

HAVE YOU TALKED TO LEIRA YET? ASKED GRANNY.

About what?

She wants you to spend the night again.

I didn't mind—Leira Chrisler made good dinners. She was lonely, had been lonely for a long time, since her husband Joe died. When I thought of Joe, I mainly remembered his mouth, a hard line with a tiny perfectly trimmed mustache running above it. He was thin, what everybody called wiry, and was always dressed fit for a funeral, people said. Every morning he got up early to walk to the bank, and late in the afternoons I would sometimes see him coming home with his dark suit and briefcase. Even in the hottest weather, he kept his suit coat on, striding resolutely along in 90° heat like he wasn't even hot at all.

Sometimes neighborhood children and their dogs would be playing in the street, but he always walked right by us as if we weren't even there and went on up the steps to his house, which was catty-corner from ours and sat back from the street under a giant, sweet-blooming magnolia tree. Once I went to chase a football and found myself right under his feet. I looked up and said, Hello, Mr. Chrisler! He stared at me strangely, nodded his head abruptly, and turned away. I never ventured to speak to him again.

Then a couple of years later he got himself killed, or killed himself, most people said, because he was found on the floor of the bank with a bullet through his head and the gun lying right there next to him. Mrs. Chrisler said no, that he would never kill himself, he loved her too much, and besides he was a Christian, no, she said there must have been a robbery attempt when he was there by himself after hours and when he tried to stop the thief, he was shot down with his own gun. But nobody, not the police nor anyone else believed her, mainly because after all the gun *was* his own gun—even Mrs. Chrisler admitted that—so there was no investigation.

I smelled the roast cooking as I went up to Mrs. Chrisler's back door. I knocked politely.

Come on in, Honey, dinner's almost ready, she said.

Mrs. Chrisler entered the room in her usual flurry, and I noticed how much she looked like a child. Not that she was young, no, her dark hair was mostly gray and up on her head in a puffy bun the way older ladies fixed their hair. It's that she was tiny like a child and had big gray eyes with oversized lashes, and she had a sweet, little-girl voice. It seemed like she never stopped talking, and about nothing.

Marilyn Jane, Honey, how are you today, she began, and without waiting to hear, she continued, I declare today has been a real work day for me, the leaves under that tree have needed raking for so long, and today was the day, I said to myself, I raked until my arms were sore, and then the bulbs in the front beds had to be taken out of the ground and stored in the garage, I'm telling you, I got so tired, I thought I would die, I just had to stop and fix myself a pitcher of lemonade, would you like a glass, Marilyn Jane, I saved some for you. With hardly a pause, she put ice in a glass for me, and kept on, How is your grandmother, Honey, I saw her this morning and she said her blood pressure was up again, I don't see how she manages with all of you children at her age, she is a saint, if anyone is . . .

The table was set with blue place mats and blue and white napkins to match. That matching thing was typical of Mrs. Chrisler—everything in her house was as it should be, all in place, and clean. She continued to talk through the roast beef, through the mashed potatoes, okra, and sliced tomatoes. Straight through the pecan pie she talked, and through the washing of the dishes.

After dinner we watched TV together, and Mrs. Chrisler cut back on the talking. She loved *The Lawrence Welk Show*. When it came on, she squealed, Isn't he the best looking *thing?* and hugged her knees up to herself. The bubble machine started, and her wide lips spread into a smile that reached across her face. She rocked in her chair, with her flannel gown covered in pink rosebuds snuggled close around her.

After the TV was shut off, she crawled into her double bed, and I lay down on the single bed next to hers. That's when she would start talking about Mr. Chrisler. You never knew him, I know she said, he wasn't much of a talker, but he was good to me. He was good to our boy, too, though Alexander never could get close to his daddy, he said, and to this day doesn't want to talk about him. He was a strict father, but it was all for the good, look at Alex now, a medical doctor, one of the best, he was right up there at the top of his class, and if it hadn't been for his father making him study the way he did—he never was allowed to go out and fritter his time away like other children—he never would have excelled the way he has. I do wish he would come home once in a while, though, he's so busy, he doesn't get much of a chance, he says. He sends me a beautiful gift every Christmas. Did you see my new Mix-Master? That came from Alex.

I miss Joe, I do, especially at night, it's not easy for a woman to be alone. He was never too demanding on me, you know, Marilyn Jane, it's hard for a woman to take a man more than twice in one night, and he never pushed me more than that, never.

I wasn't sure exactly what Mrs. Chrisler meant, but I figured it must have something to do with sex. Twice in one night? How often do people usually do it? And talking about sex as "demanding" was confusing, too. Isn't sex something two people do together because they want to, because they're in love? But I was afraid to ask Mrs.

Chrisler, afraid I would say the wrong thing. I didn't know the right words to use.

You have all of that ahead of you, Marilyn Jane, you're a lucky girl, you know, she said.

I didn't think of myself in any sense of the word as "lucky"—in fact, I wondered why people are born and why they have to hurt so much and why they have to watch other people die and then die themselves. It didn't seem like a good plan, overall. Who was I to question God, and yet I did have these questions worrying at me. Why did Joe Chrisler have to kill himself and leave Leira alone? Why is Big Papa so nervous and so mean to people? Why did my basketball coach have an affair with a married woman and get beat up and have to leave town, just at the beginning of the season? Why does Daddy drink so much? Why do I wake up sad every day?

I asked Mrs. Chrisler, Why does it have to be this way? Life, I mean? Why is it so hard for people?

Leira stopped smiling, and her eyes grew big and glossy. Her long lashes blinked, and blinked again. Something ragged caught at her throat, and she couldn't speak for a while. Finally a voice came from her, but it was not like her little-girl, squeally voice, it was a much lower voice than I had ever heard come from her. She said, We can't know the answer to questions like that, Marilyn. We have to accept what is given to us, and go on living as best we can. She paused. Marilyn Jane, you're deep, you're a very deep thinker. There are times, though, when we can't understand, and we just have to go on faith. Remember that, Honey. There are times when faith is all we've got.

I lay awake, thinking. Faith? Faith in what? Faith that things would get better? Sometimes things don't, or can't. Mr. Chrisler's not coming back, and Mrs. Chrisler will just get older and she won't be able to work in the yard or cook roast or even care about seeing Lawrence Welk. She'll get lonelier and sicker and finally die, the way Miss Gerhardt did across the street, Miss Gerhardt of the winding braids and musty books. Faith in that? Faith that God has a reason for all of the pain people suffer? If God has a reason, the least He could do is to let us in on it—otherwise, it all seems so useless. Brother Skelton says God is love. Well, if that's true, then why do we have to hurt so much?

CHAPTER 17

in which I wonder if I'm pretty

Shreveport is only fifty miles away, but I have never been there. I read the *Shreveport Times* every day, and look at all the ads. The Sunday paper has the most ads. I dream about going to one of the big department stores like Rosenberg's and buying some clothes: skirts that would show off my curves, sweaters that would fall softly over my breasts. Shreveport!

I've been making my own clothes on Granny's old treadle sewing machine since I was in the eighth grade. But they have that homemade look. I want something from one of the fancy stores in the city.

I run my fingers through the newly ironed clothes—two dresses and a couple of skirts and blouses—hanging on a metal rack on the door of Daddy's bedroom. I am picking out something to wear for prayer meeting. Daddy is propped up in bed reading *True Detective* and smoking a Picayune. What about this? I ask, holding up a navy blue print dress with white rickrack. He doesn't answer.

Daddy, what about this?

What about what? he asks, never looking up.

What about wearing this to prayer meeting tonight.

Fine, he says, still not raising his eyes.

You're not even looking, I say. Look. Would this be good?

You always look good, Sis. Don't worry about it.

I sigh. Daddy, do you think I'm pretty?

He keeps reading the magazine. Sure you're pretty, Sis. Pretty as a picture.

No, I'm not. My face is all broken out, and I'm skinny, and my hips are too big.

He looks up from his magazine at last. They always get caught in the end, he muses.

Daddy, I'm trying to talk to you.

You are pretty, Hon. Why, you were the prettiest baby I ever saw. Everybody wanted to hold you.

I don't mean when I was a baby, I mean now. I'm not pretty now. Look at these bumps on my face.

Don't worry about your face. It'll clear up in a few years. It's just a part of growing up. That's what he always says. Everything is "just a change of life," according to Daddy.

I take the dress into the bathroom and hold it in front of me as I look into the mirror. *I have a figure like a Grapette bottle. That's what Daddy said once.* Ugly, ugly, ugly, I say aloud, to the frowning face. You're ugly, and you'll always be ugly, and nobody will ever love you. Just at that moment I wish for my mother. Not really my mother, but a mother.

I return to my room and fall on my back on the bed, arms stretched out kind of like I'm flying, staring at the ceiling. I could be wrong about life, I think. Maybe it isn't all sadness and trouble. Things change.

I am twenty-four instead of fourteen. My skin is perfect, and I have on a brilliant emerald-green dress and high heels and carry a purse to match. The billowing collar of the dress frames my long graceful neck, setting off my classical features. As I walk down the crowded city sidewalk, men and women alike turn their heads to notice and part on either side to let me pass. I am tall, elegant, standing above them all. I smile as though I know a secret. I turn from their eyes and enter the door of a fine restaurant. My man is waiting for me inside. His face brightens as he sees me. Hello, Darling! he says.

Hearing the hall clock strike, I jump up from the bed. I consider my options. The navy blue with rickrack, I decide. That's the best.

CHAPTER 18

in which I fall in love for the first time

There is a first time for everyone to fall in love, I suppose. For me, it happened one day in band practice: desire struck me unaware, and I developed a long and fierce attachment to Henry Skelton, the Baptist preacher's son. Henry played last chair second trumpet, and I played first chair, third. The stage was crowded, and I soon found Henry's left thigh pressed tightly against my right thigh as we played "Stars and Stripes Forever." Soon, for no apparent reason, my right thigh began to feel warm, and then strange waves of heat began to travel from there, all through my body. My heart started pounding wildly. My face was flushed, and so was Henry's—but of course he was playing his instrument, and his face was always flushed when he played. *Does he want me, the way I want him? How could it be any other way? Aren't my feelings just an answer to a call coming from him?*

Ever since seventh grade, I had admired the sun-streaked blond hair which Henry pushed back constantly from his blue eyes. His face was as fair as a young child's, and the blush on his cheeks reminded me of the rosy color on green apples when they ripen high up in the tree.

Henry used to kid around with me. One day he pulled loose the sash on my dress and then ducked low so I wouldn't see him when I whirled around. He laughed and said, Hi, Marilyn—hey, did you know your sash is undone? And in summer at the swimming pool, he would rise from unseen depths to splash me and grin and dive down again. Seventh grade stuff, though. Now we were ninth graders.

Henry certainly never indicated that his feelings for me resembled mine for him. He never held my hand, never asked me to go to the movies with him, and never even sat by me on the band bus. He had stopped teasing me long ago, and the last thing I could remember his saying to me was, Why don't you stand up straight, one day when the marching band was practicing. He did, however, keep his left thigh firmly pressed against my right thigh during band every day at fifth period. That was enough. I was in love.

I tried to pray about my feelings. But every time I started, I felt a stone wall come up between God and me. I didn't know why the wall came, but it rose up so dark and hard that I knew it was real. God did not want to discuss the matter at all.

I figured that getting a boyfriend was part of growing up: you get to a certain age, and then a boyfriend comes along, the way your period comes along. I decided to check out this notion by asking Sarah Suther, a senior girl I knew, who her boyfriend was. Sarah of the thick glasses, Sarah of the horse-face, Sarah of the flat chest. If Sarah had a boyfriend, then anyone could get one. Trying to be casual, I sidled up to her one day in the cafeteria line, and posed the question. Sarah's answer was straightforward and unequivocal: I don't have one. I've never had one. I fell into a panic at her response. *Maybe I'll never have a boyfriend. Maybe I'll always be alone.*

The next year Henry's father was called to a bigger church in Pascagoula, Mississippi, and the family moved away. I didn't forget him, though. I kept the white gardenia that the head deacon had pinned on his lapel at the special goodbye reception First Baptist gave for the family. Actually, I retrieved it from the trashcan, where he had thrown it on his way out of the church. For two more years, I kept it on the bulletin board in my bedroom, where the flower became browner and smaller with each passing month. It was the dearest thing I owned. I thought about Henry often.

I just wish he had said goodbye. He probably just forgot.

CHAPTER 19

in which I allow myself to dream

I SLIPPED OFF TO THE BATHROOM, THE ONLY PLACE THAT WAS PRIVATE, AND even that was not completely safe, for if I stayed too long, someone— usually Big Papa, who had weak kidneys—would be there, banging on the door, demanding to be let in.

Somehow, I felt scared almost all the time, like something bad was about to happen. I would jump at a shadow on the street, and then realize it was only the darkness I myself was casting. But on this night the house was quiet, everyone in bed but me, and so I was allowed the pleasure of silence. The old claw-foot tub was deep, and I filled it with warm water. As I soaked there, I felt the stiffness in my shoulders and back easing, my neck letting go. I lay back and listened to the dribble of hot water that kept the tub always warm. Maybe this is the way it'll be when I grow up, I thought. Maybe I'll have my own tub and as much hot water as I want anytime I want it, and I won't have to answer to anyone. Maybe I won't be afraid all the time.

And as I soaked in the warmth, I let my dreams be dreamt. I dreamed of a cottage with a front porch and a swing, of daisies lining the flowerbeds, of a great grassy yard, and of a big shady oak stretching its arms over the front of the house. I dreamed of a husband who was tall and well built, a man of good character who would love me. And because of this good man's love for me, I too would be known as good, as a woman whose name was "more precious than rubies," the way the *Bible* said. And this good man would hold me in his arms and tell me I am good and tell me I am beautiful, and I would see his own beauty and goodness and so would not doubt what he said of me, and so long as he was with me, I would be safe and unafraid.

I sighed and rose out of the water, reaching for a thin towel, imagining it larger and exceedingly fluffy, and I dried my body, thinking that tonight, yes, I am slim and lovely. Reaching the towel to my back, I felt the roughness of it scratch pleasantly, and then I rubbed my breasts, making them tingle, making the nipples stand up and harden. My breasts were bigger, *noticeably* bigger, I thought. I pulled Granny's old cast-off gown, a silky peach-colored one, over my head and stood to look at my image in the mirror. I saw that I was really very pretty without my thick glasses. My brown eyes looked large and melty, and my brown hair was waving and curling round my face with the moisture. I saw a softness, a blooming, which was new for me.

I smiled, and the image smiled back at me. I tried it again, and again the pretty girl in the steamy mirror smiled back. I rolled my shoulders seductively and lowered my lashes as I smiled this time. Then I reached down and pulled up the right side of my gown, exposing the length of my long leg. I pointed my toe and swung back on my hip, the way I had seen Jane Russell do in the movies. Suddenly embarrassed, I dropped the edge of my gown and looked back in the mirror and saw a shy girl with questioning eyes. I wonder, I asked myself, if I will ever, ever be kissed. I smiled and sighed and thought, Yes, that might be possible. That just might be possible for me one day.

I was fifteen, and I did not know that I would be kissed for the first time when I was nineteen, and that the kiss would come from a tall, intellectual math major at the college I attended, and that the kiss would take place in a parked automobile—his father's Dodge—in front of the ancient brick dormitory where I lived and that the kiss would be sloppy wet and wiggly and too hard and altogether unsatisfactory. I recorded this momentous event in my journal.

Dear Journal,

Well, it finally happened, after all these years—I got kissed last night!!! By Danny Temple!! I really like him, as he is interesting to talk to, and very tall! I am so happy. The kiss was unusual, though. But how do I know, having never before been kissed? Maybe it will get better.

And kissing did get better. And I was desired by men. And that's not the whole story. But how's a girl of fifteen to know?

CHAPTER 20

in which I have my first date

IT'S FOR YOU, SIS, AND IT'S A **BOY**! HIS HAND OVER THE MOUTHPIECE, Jim handed the phone over to me.

Probably just my lab partner asking about homework, I thought as I reached for the phone, though my breath caught. Hello? I said in a kind of cracked whisper.

Hello, said the male voice on the other end of the line. He paused and coughed. Hello, he said again.

Who is this? I asked.

Uh, Roger. From down the street. Roger Wright.

Oh, hi. *Why in the world would Roger be calling me?*

Hi, Roger repeated. Uh, I wondered, I was wondering . . . A pause again, this time a long one. Would you like to go to the Valentine dance next Saturday night?

Then I became the one who couldn't speak. *Roger Wright? Why Roger Wright? Have all my dreams and prayers yielded up only Roger Wright?*

Finally Roger spoke again. Are you there, Marilyn?

Yeah, sure. I'm here. My brain raced along, computing my options. To go, or not to go. To miss this dance, like all the others, or to not miss it. To start dating, or to not start dating. To keep waiting, or to go with what destiny had thrown in my lap—a dilemma that was to be repeated all too often in future decisions about men.

Yeah, I'd like to go. To the dance, I mean.

OK. I'll pick you up at 8:00. OK?

OK.

My OK held such a question, that Roger felt he should ask again, OK? You sure you want to go?

Sure. OK. Yes, I do.

Roger would probably be a famous physicist one day, I figured. He was no doubt the brightest boy in Homer High. The problem was the way he looked. He had glasses so thick that they distorted his eyes, fair skin covered with pimples, and posture so bad that his neck stuck out from his round shoulders like a turtle's. At least he was tall. I wouldn't have to dance with somebody a foot shorter, the way it happened in the dance classes I had taken.

Daddy bought me a shimmery blue taffeta dress with a full gathered skirt for the occasion. The light played on it when I twirled around in front of the store mirror. I got new shoes, too— black suede, with rhinestones on the toes. On the afternoon of the dance, the delivery truck from the florist arrived with a corsage: white carnations with a pink pipe cleaner heart perched on top. We danced, if that's what you want to call it. His body was absolutely rigid, and so I had to do all the leading, pushing him around the floor. One, two, back-step, one, two, back-step.

The other couples were whirling and laughing all around us, having a good time. Everybody was looking at us. We looked so stupid. All this color, and I was in a black pit with Roger Wright. After each dance, each and every one, he said thank you and shook my hand. His hands were soft and sweaty, and they trembled. To make things worse, each time he shook my hand, he then stepped back and pulled out a huge white handkerchief—the biggest handkerchief I had ever seen—and blew his nose, loudly, right there in the middle of the dance floor. Finally I told him I had to be home early because of church the next day.

I knew that Marguerite would ask on Monday. She was beating the cornbread batter for supper. The big iron skillet with its red-hot bacon grease was smoking on the stove.

How wuz the dance, Miss Marilyn? Did you have a good time?

No, Marguerite, I had a terrible time. I had an awful time. I had the worst time of my life. Roger is such a . . . such a . . .

Marguerite kept on with her steady beating. He be jes growin' up, jes like you, Miss Marilyn. It ain't easy, Honey.

Marguerite, will I ever have a boyfriend—a real boyfriend? Tears slid out the corners of my eyes as I sat there on the kitchen stool, my elbows on my knees, my hands under my chin. I mean, somebody I *like*?

The cornbread sizzled into the skillet. Then Marguerite turned, the bowl still in her hands, and looked at me straight on. Ain't you the strangest thing? O' course you will, Honey. You gettin' prettier every day, and that's no lie. Has Marguerite ever tol' you a story? She popped the cornbread in the oven and then moved to the sink, rinsing out the bowl. You gonna have all the boyfriends you want, and more prob'ly than you want to put up wif, you mark my words.

More than I want to put up with? What could Marguerite mean? If I could just have one that I liked, that would be good. That would be enough. I would be satisfied. Forever. I wouldn't want for anything else, I swear Jesus I wouldn't. Ever. Just don't send me any more Roger Wrights, please don't. I can't take any more like that.

CHAPTER 21

in which I learn about marriage

BIG PAPA AND GRANNY ARE PLAYING DOMINOES AGAIN ON THE FRONT porch. Big houseflies are floating through the air like tiny gliders, lighting on the two players and on the card table and on the rocking chairs, just like they own the place. I'm glad for the big oak tree that spreads its branches over the porch and the front yard, keeping the worst of the heat away. Every once in a while, what you might call a breeze blows, but it generally just moves the warm air around a little.

I'm reading *A Man for Marcy*, by Rosamond du Jardin. I've read *Double Date*, and all the other books she's written. Marcy is a high school senior and her boyfriend Steve is going off to college. She tells him he'll probably forget about her, but he says no, never: "Marcy felt Steve's arm tighten around her and her heart quickened as she lifted her lips for his kiss. . . . 'I couldn't forget you if I tried,' Steve told her, his voice low and not quite steady. 'You're the one, Marce. You always will be.'"

Mama-dog is here, too, lying on the concrete porch next to me, her tongue hanging out, panting from the heat. I can smell the talcum powder that Papa uses to make the table smooth and slick. Whenever he shuffles the dominos, tiny clouds of powder rise from the table, and that sweet scent wafts out to me. We're all drinking sweet tea out of tall sweating glasses.

Big Papa is cheating on the points, as he always does when he is behind. He can't stand to lose, especially to a woman. Granny never calls his hand when he does this—she knows he will get his dander up if she does, so instead she takes to talking about her former suitors. It's her way.

I wonder whatever became of Edward, she says. My, oh, my how that boy did love me. Big Papa doesn't say anything, just looks hard at his dominoes and considers his choices. Papa taps his fingers on the table. He plays, makes five points, and records ten on his wooden counter.

I go back to my book. Steve has come home for his first visit: "Marcy's insides were a quivering mass of hope and uncertainty as she went down the carpeted stairs. Quietly she pursued the sound of voices along the hallway, wanting one glimpse of Steve before he saw her."

Granny sings softly, In the sweet by and by, we shall meet on that beautiful shore . . . and plays the double six, for fifteen points. She records the points on her counter.

Yes, he did. For a fact. He wanted so bad to marry me.

Big Papa clears his throat. Will you be quiet, Mama, and let me think, he says. He takes one ivory domino in his right hand and turns it over and over on the table as he tries to decide his next play. He plays, putting the domino down extra hard. No points this time. Granny is still humming the hymn.

I read on: "His hands reached out and pulled her close to him and his lips met hers in a short kiss that made Marcy's pulse pound and sent hot color to her cheeks."

Everybody said I should have paid him some attention, but I was stuck on you, Granny says. He told me I was the prettiest girl he had ever seen. Well, that's what they all said—that I was the prettiest girl in five counties. You know, when I was twenty-one years old, my waist measured twenty-one inches. She plays, for five more points.

Big Papa's frown grows deeper. He concentrates on the game, and swats hard at a fly that's buzzing round his head. He is forced to draw, once, twice, and on the third time, he is able to play. Ha! he says. He makes ten points, and records fifteen.

Granny has just two dominoes left, and she plays one of those, for no score. She continues about Edward. They say he made a lot of money. In the lumber business. He always had his head about him, that's one thing for sure. And he came from a good family. You can't fault them.

She's really asking for it.

Mama, will you hush! A man can't hardly think straight with all that jabbering, Papa says. His eyes scan all the possibilities on the board. He looks down at his row of dominoes. He looks back at the board, his eyes narrowing. He draws four times, finally finding one he can play. No points.

Domino! Granny says, as she plays her final piece. I'm thinking, now there'll be the devil to pay. Sure enough. Even Mama-dog perks up her ears. She knows when a row is coming.

Papa knocks his dominoes face down and pushes them to the center of the board, scattering the other pieces. This is the last time I'm playing with you, Mama! Lord-o'-mercy, if you can't keep your mouth shut, how can I think what I'm doing? He stalks inside, slamming the screen door behind him. Granny puts the dominoes into their worn cardboard box, still humming "Sweet By and By." She puts away the wooden counting boards and the pegs. She knows he will be back tomorrow for another game. She'll let him win, and he'll be all right. She ought to let this Edward thing go, though, I think.

Granny, how did you meet Big Papa? I ask, putting down my book. Why did you want to marry him?

She rocks in her chair and looks off down the street. Well, I tell you, Honey, you never know a man until you live with him. Courtship is different. A man always puts his best foot forward.

She continues to rock. She drinks slowly from her glass of iced tea. Now your Papa had his eye on my sister—saw her at a dance. But then a friend of his told him, If you think *she* is pretty, you should see her sister. So he came calling the next day, and I reckon he liked what he saw. They all said I was the prettiest girl in five counties, you know.

I wish I had known her when she was young and pretty. Now she's mostly tired.

But why did you marry him?

Like I said, he put his best foot forward. Nothing was too good for me. That first day he came to my father, and spoke right up. Mr. Honeycutt, I'd like to take Gertie for a ride, if you don't mind, Sir. My father liked his polite manner, I think. Your Papa was a young man then, don't forget. He was handsome, tall, with a blonde moustache. He had a beautiful team of horses pulling his wagon, too, a sorrel and a dappled gray. I can still see that pair. He proposed before long, and I accepted.

She has stopped rocking, she is staring at nothing in particular. She is holding her iced tea, the ice almost melted now, rivulets running down the outside of the glass.

Then did you get married right away? I ask, reaching down to scratch Mama-dog's ear. Mama-dog stretches and wags her tail.

No, she said, coming back to the present. We had long engagements in those days. I was engaged for a year before we married. And mind you during that time, we respected each other. Not like young people nowadays.

She falls silent for a moment. I remember once when we were sitting on the front porch of my daddy's house swinging in our old swing, she says. It was dusk and nobody else was around. Your Papa leaned over and asked me if I would kiss him. I of course said no. Later he told me that if I had allowed him to do that, he never would have married me—he wouldn't have respected me enough, he said. My mother always told me, Never let a man get close enough to touch the hem of your garment. I think that's still good advice for young people.

Never let a man get close enough to touch the hem of your garment? And here I am, every day, dreaming about my first kiss. When will it ever come? Granny doesn't know I have these thoughts, and how often I have them. I pat Mama-dog's head, and go back to my book.

Steve has told Marcy that he has been dating someone else at college: "We agreed before I left that we'd both have dates with other people. You know we did, Marce. . . . Marcy felt anger boil up in her like a geyser getting ready to erupt. . . . Words poured from Marcy's mouth, furious, resentful words. She told Steve just what she thought of him. She accused him of pretending to like her and sneaking behind her back to date another girl. She called him fickle and said he had deceived her. . . . The upshot was that Marcy insisted on being taken home at once. And Steve, tight-lipped and glaring, complied with her demand. They parted wordlessly, with only the hard slam of the car door. . . ."

I sigh. Does love always have to be so . . . difficult?

CHAPTER 22

in which I find myself unworthy

SURPRISE! A CHORUS OF VOICES GREETED ME AS I OPENED THE SCREEN door to Mamie Endom's house. Happy Birthday!

To get me there, Mamie had called to say she was cooking and needed another egg and could she borrow one, and so I went on down the street with the egg, never expecting something like a birthday party. Other people had birthday parties, but I did not. At least, not since we left Mother.

I knew I should have been happy, and I started smiling the way I thought I should, but I felt embarrassed—no, more than embarrassed, I felt mortified. I was sure I didn't deserve this kind of attention. I was the one who always sat on the end when the group went to the movies. I longed to sit in the middle, to be the one chosen, but that was not my part.

Yet here they were, gathered together for me—Grace and Ellis Ann and Peggy and all the others—and Mamie's kitchen decorated with streamers, and paper hats and colored napkins on the table and a huge white sheet cake with pink rosebuds and green leaves and "Happy Birthday, Marilyn!" written all the way across it. I couldn't say anything at all. Mamie was grinning, her round cheeks flushed bright red.

You didn't know, did you, Marilyn, nobody told you?

No, I didn't know, I said in a voice scarcely above a whisper, trying all the while to keep the smile on my face. This is . . . just wonderful.

And the chatter of the party began. I felt detached from the talk, unable to follow what people were saying. Bits of various conversations drifted by.

Elvis is coming to Shreveport in September! Yeah, the Louisiana Hay Ride. Can you believe that? Elvis! We have to go hear him.

Old Bird-legs gave us the hardest French test yesterday—I can't stand that woman.

Do you think he likes me now, he used to like Susan, and she still likes him, she wants to know if he still likes her, but I don't know what to tell her.

The hardest part was opening the presents. Each girl had brought a gift, and each gift had to be opened and exclaimed over and then passed around to the rest of the guests for inspection. I went about the task carefully, keeping my eyes low, tugging gently at the tape, trying not to tear any of the paper, trying not to let my friends see the tremble in my hands. A silk neck scarf, a jangling charm bracelet, a real leather billfold—each gift had been chosen for me, and I knew I was supposed to feel thankful, but I could not. I was unworthy. I smiled, I said the right things, I hoped they wouldn't notice the darkness in my eyes.

Listening to them sing "Happy Birthday" made me squirm inside, especially the ending: Happy birthday, Dear Marilyn, happy birthday to you! I knew I wasn't dear to any of them. I was the one with the answers in class, I was the leader of the clubs, the feature editor of the school newspaper, but dear to them, I was not. I knew that beyond a doubt. I blew out the candles and made my wish: *Oh, God, let me somehow grow into a person who can be loved.* It was a prayer more than a wish, but I guess wishing is close kin to praying.

I hoped they would go home soon. The cake was eaten, the conversation wound down, and at last my ordeal was over. I smiled and said thank you to each of them and thank you to Mamie over and over. No one had ever before done anything like this for me, and how someone who was just the next-door neighbor could care so much for me, I couldn't understand.

Mamie gave me a Jitney-Jungle bag to put all the gifts in, and I went home and hid all the things in the bottom drawer of my little blue chest of drawers because I knew Donna would be getting into them if I didn't, and then I lay down on the bed, exhausted, and let the tears come. I wondered why I was such a strange person, not able to accept love even when it was plunked right down in my lap? Why was I even born, if it was to live like this?

Thinking back, I wonder what drew me forward. I believe it was only a nameless sense that things might not always be this way. Despair was an option, I suppose, but not a good one. I bet on hope. God might surprise me, like in the Bible, *whoosh*, angel's wings appear from nowhere and people's lives are turned around. Why not give God a chance, because in this world you never really know what might happen next.

CHAPTER 23

in which Big Papa almost kills my brother Jim

BIG PAPA'S IMAGINARY CANCER BOTHERED HIM A LOT. HE SENT LOTS OF money off to the Hoxsey Cancer Clinic over the years, an outfit established in 1936 in Dallas, Texas, that treated cancer with herbs and ointments. The FDA shut them down in 1960, and they moved to Tijuana—but not before they made millions and established 17 centers around the country.

I can understand why Papa picked cancer for his disease of choice, because everybody in the family pretty much dies of cancer—all my six aunts and uncles, all the Fulmer progeny except my father, who died of alcohol dementia.

Anyway, I guess Big Papa heard the Hoxsey clinic advertised on J. Harold Smith's *Radio Gospel Bible Hour* out of Del Rio, Texas, because that's the only station he ever listened to. I think Big Papa was partial to J. Harold because Papa was convinced he would be punished for the sins of his youth—never mind the sins of his adulthood, like beating all his children and being an all-round arrogant and mean-spirited human being.

Papa would get downright morose about this sinning business. He would take his head in his hands and start moaning and groaning, rocking back and forth in his big chair. Then he would get into his cancer thing: I've got cancer, he would wail, I know I have. It won't be long now. I won't be in this world much longer.

Some days it would get worse. Sometimes I feel so bad, so nervous,

Big Papa would say, that I just want to go in there in the back bedroom and get the shotgun off the wall and blow my brains out.

That always scared me, when Papa said that, because I thought he might do it one day. I thought what it would be like, hearing the gun go off in the middle of the night, and how my heart would jump, and how I would go to the back bedroom and see him there lying in a big puddle of blood, half of his head blown off, and his guilty eyes staring at me. I'd be the one who'd have to go see about him. I'd have to call the ambulance, and take care of Granny and Jim and Donna. Big Papa wouldn't do it when Daddy was home, because Daddy slept in the back bedroom where the guns were hanging. In any case, no, he'd wait until Daddy was gone, so I'd have to take care of everything.

Most nights Papa was more or less calm, though, and we got to watch TV. We saw *The Hit Parade* and *Dragnet*. Right after *Gunsmoke*, he made us go to bed because that's when he went to sleep. I wanted to stay up and read, but lights had to be out at 9:00, because he didn't want us running up the electric bill, he said.

One night a noise woke me up. It was Papa's voice, shouting at somebody. I got up and followed the sound and there was Big Papa holding the shotgun on Jim.

What happened was that my brother Jim came home late that night, around 12:30 or so, and Papa, thinking he was already home, took my brother for an intruder. Papa came within an inch of shooting him. My own brother could have been dead. Yes, Jim could have lost his life. Because of Big Papa's craziness. It was one thing for him to kill himself—there was grain of sense in that—but it would be another thing altogether for him to kill Jim, as sweet a boy as you would ever know.

꧁

CHAPTER 24

in which I am afraid of falling

LIKE ALL HIGH SCHOOLS OF MY DAY, EVERY YEAR WE PRODUCED A SCHOOL yearbook with pictures of the classes, the clubs, the athletic teams, and of course the awards for qualities like Most Beautiful and Most Popular. When I was a senior, I got two awards: Miss Betty Crocker Future Homemaker of the Year and Most Intelligent. I got the Betty Crocker award because of a test I took that asked questions like where do you place the dessert spoon when you set the table and how many stitches to the inch do you use when sewing silk. I figured I got the Most Intelligent award because all the people smarter than me got better kinds of awards like Most Likely to Succeed or Miss Homer High. That year I was also awarded Best Christian at the First Baptist church, probably because I had never been able to get a boyfriend.

꧁

It was Sunday night after youth fellowship. The church gang all piled in the car to go riding around.

Let's go climb the fire tower! Carolyn shouted, and we were off. Tommy had his daddy's big Pontiac. There was room for two couples in the back seat, and Barbara Sue and I climbed in the front with Tommy.

On our way to the thick forest where the fire tower rose against the sky, the couples in the back seat had a kissing contest. Whoever kissed the longest without coming up for air won. I heard the sounds, and I caught a glance of the couples whenever I could. I felt a slick wetness come in my panties, and I wondered what it would be like to kiss this way.

We reached the site, and Tommy pulled off the road and stopped the car. We were surrounded by the deepest darkness. Without the engine's noise the only sounds came from the frogs and crickets.

Last one up's a rotten egg! yelled Tommy, and everybody scrambled out and began racing up the tower, squealing with laughter. Everybody but me, that is. I stayed in the car, as always. Somebody had to stay with the car, I reasoned. But I knew that wasn't the truth. I wanted to run, wanted to climb like the others, but I was afraid of falling.

CHAPTER 25

in which I find a place of acceptance

MAYBE THE MOST DISCONCERTING THING ABOUT GROWING UP IN HOMER, Louisiana, was the overwhelming and ever present sense that I was different from other people—kind of like a broccoli plant that slipped into the row of cauliflower, or a duck in the chicken yard. Some differences were clear and decisive: my mother was missing, my father was an alcoholic in a town that was dry, and I lived with my elderly grandparents. Divorce was a concept that hadn't reached Louisiana in the 1950's, so I knew no one else from a "broken home." I didn't dare invite other kids over, because I never knew when Daddy would be drunk or my grandfather in one of his dark moods.

By the time I was thirteen, I was taller than all of the girls in my class and some of the boys, and besides that, I was a teen introvert who would rather read books than be with people. I now see that I was carrying a load of grief that I didn't understand and couldn't articulate. So much was going on inside, unacknowledged and unspoken, that I didn't have the wherewithal to be interested in others.

Today I would have been called "depressed," but that word hadn't come into common usage, so I just thought I was sad by nature. Until you can name something, it doesn't exist. I'm no longer depressed, but I am still more comfortable with melancholy than joy—and always and ever, "cheerful" has been an abomination to me. Men still stop me on the street from time to time and say something like, Why don't you smile, pretty lady?

I scowl and I think, Fuck you.

As I navigated my way through my teens, I began to be aware of some strengths. I knew I was fairly smart and that I was a leader— this I learned at school and at church—but these qualities are not the most coveted by an adolescent girl. I longed to be wanted, to be chosen.

Don't we all just want to be loved?

At the same time, I knew that Homer, Louisiana, was not the center of the universe. I sensed that there were places where I might fit better, might possibly be admired, or even liked. I couldn't imagine being loved, but maybe *liked* I could hope for. From my books, I knew there were other people who were thirsty to learn.

Although neither my father or my mother ever finished high school, my extended family respected learning, valued education. Big Papa had attended a "normal school," one of the early teacher-training institutions. The name fell out of favor toward the end of the 1920's, and these schools changed their name to "teachers colleges," today's equivalent of state colleges. My grandfather had risen to the respectable position of postmaster of our town. The street we lived on, Fulmer Street, was named after him. Big Papa reminded us three children regularly, Get your education. They can't take that away from you. This was a message about social class, as much as it was about education.

He had imbued his own children as well with that message, for four of the seven finished college, two with master's degrees and one, Uncle Lemos, with a Ph.D. Lemos Fulmer served for a time as the head of the Education Department at Louisiana State University. He was a blustery conservative whose tenure in the position was cut short when it was reported in the Shreveport *Times* and subsequently in national news services that he prevented a young man from entering the School of Education at LSU because the man "had a red beard." My uncle was quoted as saying, "This is not the type of person we want teaching our children."

There was no question that Jim and Donna and I would all go

to college—and would finish our studies. Had someone been paying attention to the matter, I would likely have gone to LSU, because of my love of literature and my desire to become a teacher. That choice didn't occur to anyone in my family, or to me. The act of leaving Homer was itself momentous, and money was tight, so I opted for Louisiana Polytechnic, the college that was closest and cheapest.

My father's work was off and on—he was called when an oil company needed him to bring in a well—but he was an excellent hand and so managed to work fairly regularly. We three kids never doubted that we would be able to pay our tuition and room and board. Not one to trust banks, Daddy stashed away cash in the bottom drawer of his chest of drawers, tucking the bills into a worn leather pouch. The pouch was a gift from Grandma Honeycutt, Granny's mother, whom I never knew, of course, but whom Daddy revered. I gathered that she was a refuge from Big Papa's harsh parenting. She gave Daddy a lucky rabbit foot when he was a boy, a talisman that stayed in the pouch and kept our money safe.

I was right about the world beyond Homer: when I arrived at college, I found lots of people like me, people who were drawn to books and learning. My professors loved having me in class, because I sat in the front row and eagerly scarfed up whatever they were handing out. I was curious about the squirming paramecium, amazed at John Brown's raids, and loved the beauty and exactness of geometry. College was an oasis of living water for me, and I could drink as much as I wanted, all the time.

Best of all, boys started asking me out. Louisiana Tech was known as an engineering school, and so a multitude of young men with slide rules could be seen walking around the campus, and the ratio of men to women was favorable.

The summer before college, in preparation for my new life, I got rid of my thick glasses and got contact lenses, the first ones in Homer. Dr. Woodall, the opthamologist, had to read the accompanying instructions in order to see how I should insert the lenses. I earned the money for my contacts by wheedling a typing job at the Abstract Office, where deeds were prepared—I was slow, but I was accurate, dependable, and dirt-cheap. I think I started at $40 a week. Once in contacts, I never wore glasses again. I had become a fairly skilled seamstress by then, and I made dresses with sashes and wide skirts to wear over multiple petticoats, as was the fashion of the day. I put rollers in my hair.

Soon after arriving on campus, I discovered that the upper-classmen were eagerly awaiting the new crop of freshman girls. Mike asked me to church, Dwayne asked me to a hayride. I was dating!

CHAPTER 26

in which I score a date with a BMOC

WHEN VANCE CALLED AND ASKED ME TO THE FIRST FOOTBALL GAME OF the season, I wasn't totally surprised. I could tell that he had been watching me. At a Baptist Student Union picnic, I bent over the tub of iced drinks to get a Coke, and I felt eyes on me. When I turned and looked, it was Vance. He was smiling and drinking a Coke. He lifted his bottle in the air and said Hi—that's all, but I knew he was interested. I didn't understand why, though. Vance was the most sought-after guy in the BSU—he was tall and ruggedly handsome, but unassuming. He was also deeply religious. In fact, he was planning to become a medical missionary, and that in itself was hugely appealing to BSU women. An all-around perfect guy. I could hardly say no, of course, but after accepting his invitation I fell into a vast well of anxiety and self-doubt.

I thought all week about the game, what I would wear, and how I would act. I decided on the new green sheath dress I had just made, the one with the wide belt that set off my figure. I decided to act like I loved life and people, because I knew that I was supposed to love life and people, though of course I did not. I didn't particularly like people, and life scared me. I knew I shouldn't say anything about books or ideas, because I was supposed to be having fun, not being serious, and I had always been accused of being too serious.

As soon as he picked me up, I started smiling. I tried to smile all the time, but I wasn't used to smiling so much, and so my smile muscles got tired and refused to work. When I tried to smile, my upper lip would just quiver a little and my mouth would settle back into its usual state. I let my lips rest for a while, but long before the halftime, they refused to smile anymore. They couldn't.

As for conversation, I tried to say things that fall into the "love life and people" category, but they all came out sounding phony. Of course, they *were* phony. For example, I smiled and said, Look at these gorgeous autumn leaves, don't they make you feel glad to be alive?

Vance just said Huh and not much else.

A while later I said, Isn't it great to be out here cheering for Tech, with all these great people?

He said, Yeah, it sure is.

I got this fixation on the word "great," and I kept saying it all the time, like, what a great day for this great game, and when he asked me if I wanted a Coke, I said, What a great idea, that would taste great, and the harder I tried not to say great, the more I said it, it was like I couldn't help it, like thousands of "greats" were waiting inside my mouth and every time I opened it, a few would leap out. Vance was standing up and cheering a lot, but as the game went on, I shut down more and more, I didn't want any more greats to escape, so I didn't say anything else—I just got up and cheered when Vance did, wondering how long the agony would go on.

At halftime Vance got us both hot dogs, and while I was eating on one end, the other end dropped a huge blob of mustard on my new dress, right on my left breast. I tried to wipe it off with my napkin, but that just seemed to spread the mustard even more. Vance glanced at the stain, then quickly turned his eyes away.

At last the game was over. I was glad for the chance to get up and shuffle along with the crowd, like one ant with lots of other ants, and not feel like I had to say anything. Vance put his big hand on my waist and guided me through. He was so smooth. During our walk back to my dorm, I found that I was completely out of I love life and people remarks, and all out of smiles. Vance didn't have much to say, either. He thanked me at the door for going out with him, and I said, Oh, thank *you*, Vance, it was my pleasure. I enjoyed it *so much*.

Of course, he never called me again.

CHAPTER 27

in which I get my first boyfriend

DANNY, THE TALL INTELLECTUAL MATH MAJOR, WAS THE FIRST BOY WHO ever kissed me. I didn't know why I was so attracted to him, but I was. Maybe it was the way he shifted his hips when he walked. He was lean and lanky and he sauntered through the world, every muscle moving like he was in slow motion or an underwater ballet. His eyes were big and gray-blue, with long, sleepy lashes, which he rubbed with his fist like a baby sometimes, like he was trying to wake up. When I was with him, I felt as if something was about to happen soon, some adventure, some kind of possibility.

We went to movies or to parties at First Baptist Church there in Ruston or to the A&W Drive-In on the edge of town, where we could get a frosty mug of root beer for five cents. Sometimes we just went riding around, though his dad wouldn't let him do much of that, because gasoline cost too much. Occasionally we went over to his house and played ping-pong. I thought he had the ideal family. His father had horn-rimmed glasses and a crew cut. He was the head of the math department at Tech and was as friendly as could be. Danny's mother took care of the house and Danny's three younger brothers and sisters. She was all sweetness and smiles—a tiny woman, which surprised me, because Danny was 6'4".

The two things I liked best about Danny were the talk and the kissing. We talked about religion and the meaning of life. I didn't think of myself as an intellectual at the time, but that love for big-picture, what-does-it-all-mean talk has always been a part of me. Danny was inclined that way, too. We spent a lot of time kissing, parked outside my dorm in his Daddy's car. Actually, I would have preferred to spend more time kissing and less time talking, but I didn't want to seem too forward.

In May, at the end of our junior year, he asked me to go steady, and I started wearing his class ring on a chain around my neck. Later that summer, he said he would like to drive over to Homer to visit. I had never invited anyone home with me. I wanted to tell Danny he couldn't come, but I didn't know how to say no, so I said OK. I decided to take him out to the roadside park for a picnic. Picnics are romantic, I figured. There we could talk and be alone, away from my unpredictable family.

I went out and bought a wicker picnic basket, an expensive one, the kind with flaps that open on top. I made fried chicken and potato salad, bought some fancy olives and pickles, and found some beautiful grapes that looked like they could have come right out of a magazine. Plus I made an apple pie for dessert. I even bought a red-checkered tea towel to tuck around the food, just like you would see in a movie.

But then rain came. It rained the night before Danny was to visit, and on into the morning and finally slacked off at eleven when he drove up. I invited him in, and we settled uncomfortably in the living room, a formal room that the family never used except at Christmas and Thanksgiving when the aunts and uncles came home. It smelled of decay, and the dark furniture felt almost damp to the touch. The floral wallpaper was discolored and some of it was tattered or even hanging loose on the wall. I had never much noticed the wallpaper before Danny's visit, but now I did, and I felt ashamed. It wasn't just a little feeling of I wish we had better wallpaper, no, it was more like a deep darkness that grabbed me and shook me, like I had invited him into a home that turned out to be some kind of ruin, and there was nothing I could do about it.

Then Danny asked to go to the bathroom. I should have known that was coming, he was always going to the bathroom, but I hated for him to use ours. For one thing, it was only a tiny room and there was a washing machine that took up a huge amount of space, with a hose that emptied the dirty water from Daddy's work clothes into the bathtub. The linoleum was worn out, worn completely through in places, and torn, and there was a hole about the size of a quarter in the floor next to the toilet, a hole Daddy had drilled to let the water out when the washing machine overflowed once. I didn't want Danny to see all this, it's not the way people are supposed to live. But there was no way for me to redeem the bathroom, so I just acted like nothing was wrong and showed him the way. At least it was clean, I saw to that beforehand.

When he returned, I cleared my throat and said, Well, are you hungry, Danny, I'm about ready to get out of here, what do you think?

He said yes, that he could eat, so we took off for the park with the picnic basket and some Cokes.

We had the park all to ourselves because the trees were still dripping, and the picnic tables and benches were wet. Danny had a blanket in his car that we put over the bench, so that helped. I forgot the bottle opener, and Danny tried to open a bottle on the edge of the picnic table, but that didn't work, so we didn't have anything to drink. He said it didn't matter, but I knew that it did. I started laying out the food I was so proud of, but it didn't look good to me anymore. I wasn't even hungry. I felt like this picnic was some kind of act I had to get through, pretending that I was having a good time, that I felt happy. I liked Danny, but right then I didn't like him. I just wanted him to finish his chicken and go back home.

I've never been good at hiding my feelings, so I guess I was not saying much and just picking at my food. Danny asked me if anything was wrong. What was I going to say—I don't like myself? I'm ashamed of my home? You can't say those things. So I said maybe I was coming down with something, that I didn't feel too good, and that part, the part about not feeling too good, was the truth.

So after the picnic, he dropped me and my picnic basket off at home, and said he ought to get back, his folks were expecting him. Before he left, though, he gave me a present: a miniature cedar chest with "St. Louis Cardinals" printed on top, along with a red cardinal. He said he went to a Cards game on his vacation, and he wanted me to have this little box to remember his favorite team by. I opened it and smelled the pungent odor of the cedar. For some strange reason, I felt teary, maybe because he had never given me anything before.

I wanted my relationship with Danny to last, but I began to feel the edges fraying, the fabric becoming thin. Several months later— as a matter of fact, on my birthday in July—he drove up in front of the dorm after our date and said he wanted to talk. I knew something was wrong, because that was when we usually kissed until the porch light blinked its warning, and I had to go in. I was right. Danny told me that he didn't want to go steady any longer. He said that French kissing takes too much energy. This was a surprise to me, and a very bad sign, I thought. He said he still wanted to date me, he just didn't want to be "tied down" to any one girl. But he started dating Martha Ann after that, and he stopped asking me out. She wasn't pretty, I thought—she had a funny bent nose. But she smiled a lot and had a tiny waist. And she was smart.

After Danny and I broke up, I kept opening the cedar box and taking in the smell—it was just like the woods after a rain, only better. I kept my gold medals in it, the ones I won at State Rally in home economics and English. I liked to think of them there, safe, in that little box.

When fall arrived, though, another boy entered the picture and softened my sadness over losing Danny. His name was Bill. He was President of the Baptist Student Union, and he was planning to become a doctor. Amazing! He came after me with serious intent.

CHAPTER 28

in which I learn about death

Big Papa started going downhill after Granny got her stroke. She was paralyzed and couldn't do anything except sit up in her wheel chair and look at you with those pale blue eyes, and say *wee, wee, wee*. There was nobody to take care of her except Big Papa, who was too old, and so my aunts and uncles said there was nothing else to do but put her in the nursing home out on the Minden Road.

Big Papa didn't know what to do without Mama in the house—that's what he called her, Mama—because she had never been gone from him in the sixty-seven years she had been his wife. Papa used to go downtown to the courthouse every day to play dominos, walking tall, straight, in his dress pants, with just his cane, but he stopped after Granny left.

The doctors put him in the hospital but couldn't diagnose anything except old age. It's hard to say what he died of, except missing Granny. Once he was there, all he did was smoke his Prince Albert tobacco and talk about Mama. He called to her in the night the nurses said and made such a fuss that they had to give him medicine to settle him down.

Aunt Mellie called me and told me to come on home and see Big Papa, because he wasn't doing well at all. So I drove up to Homer, drove straight to the Methodist Memorial Hospital, up by the swimming pool, and went right on in to find him. He was just filling his pipe and was sitting up in bed, a little pale and his Roman nose a little thinner maybe, but overall I thought he was looking good for somebody who was supposed to be sick enough to be in the hospital.

Hello, Marilyn Jane, he said. He was trying to find his box of matches to light his pipe and he couldn't so I went out to the nursing station to get some matches. He did look thinner, I thought, as I watched him try to draw fire into his pipe. The matches were little brittle ones with tiny red heads on them, so he couldn't get a light, he just kept scratching, scratching those matches on the box and bringing that little yellow flame up to his pipe, then having it go out when he sucked on the stem, over and over again. I was watching his attempts, but I didn't know how to help. I started feeling nervous and out of sorts because I couldn't do anything but sit there and watch those matches go out.

Finally Big Papa put down his pipe to rest a minute, and I saw a red rim around his blue eyes. I had never known him to cry, and yet when he looked up at me I saw that he had been maybe crying, his eyes were red and kept getting redder and wouldn't clear up. He looked right at me and said, I think I'm going to die, Marilyn Jane.

I took a deep breath and I thought, well of course you are, you're eighty-eight, and nobody lasts forever. But that's not what I said, because I could see that Big Papa was scared, scared deep down. So I said, you look good to me, Papa, I don't think you're doing bad at all, why I expected to see you flat out in this bed, not sitting up and smoking this way.

Then he asked me where was Mama and I tried to tell him how it was that she got sick and had to go out to the nursing home on the Minden Road. Aunt Mellie had told him that and Daddy and Uncle Gene, too, but he just couldn't understand, and so when I told him, he stared hard at me and asked when was she coming home. I knew of course that she wasn't ever coming home, but I didn't say that to Papa because I was afraid it would make him not want to live any longer, and so I just said I don't know.

But he knew anyway, I think. He said, I won't be here much longer. I knew he was going to die and I felt pity for him and I was glad I was not that old and not going to die—or if I was, I would worry about it when the occasion presented itself.

After a few minutes, I said goodbye, you really do look good, and touched his hand, which was cold and dry. That was something I never dared to do, touch him, when I was growing up, because he was so hard inside. Sure enough, he was right about dying: I never did see him alive again.

I never had seen anybody dead before, and I dreaded going to the funeral home to see his body in the casket, but of course I had to, because that's what we all did back then. When I went for the viewing, went into that sweet-smelling room, Papa wasn't even there, nothing but his shell was there, like an old snakeskin shed off. But Big Papa was gone. The blonde hair, still blonde into age, and the Roman nose, the nose he gave all his children and half his grandchildren, were there, but his flesh had turned to wax and his eyes were sewed shut, and he was gone, in spite of rosy cheeks and lips colored red, he was gone.

Big Papa was a Mason, third degree, and I had seen his gold signet ring many times but never knew what the Masons did—they were a secret organization Papa told me, and he wasn't supposed to tell anything about them. I never even knew who else in town was a Mason because I guess Papa was too old to meet with them, but every last one was there at his funeral. After the sons and grand-sons had lowered Papa's casket into the ground, the Masons came and stood round the hole and each threw a piece of cedar into the ground on top of Papa and each said in turn, From dust we come, and to dust we shall return. Big Papa, who had lorded it over us all, was flat now, and still, and one day, it occurred to me, I would be flat and still, like him.

When I got back to the house from the burial, I was so hungry that I had to have something right then, so I went right to the fridge and pulled open the door and my eyes went straight to the carcass of the chicken that Mamie Endom down the street had brought us. It was just waiting there to be finished up and so I took it for myself—well, most of the good parts were gone anyway—and I was so hungry I picked it up in my hands and started biting big mouthfuls, and gel and grease started running down my hands and onto my arms, and I—*saw Papa in his coffin*—just dripped with it but I couldn't stop, I hardly chewed it really, *I saw Papa*, and I ate even faster and finished it all, even the soft parts on the back and, *Papa there*, and the carcass was picked clean before I realized it, and I stopped and put down the cage of bones and looked at my greasy self, my arms, my dress-up dress all spotted and *Papa in his coffin was there* and I cried, for the first time since Papa died, not because I liked Papa, which I didn't, but because he was gone, and I started to know that I loved him then, which is a strange way to start loving somebody, just when he's dead, but that's the way it happened for me. You can't help loving what you get used to.

CHAPTER 29

in which I become engaged to be married

PEOPLE GET MARRIED FOR ALL KINDS OF REASONS, DON'T THEY. PERSON-
ally, I myself am getting married because Bill loves me. He lets me
know that in so many ways, like asking me what movie I prefer
or what I want to eat. He is a perfect gentleman, and respectful,
opening the car door for me and helping me with my coat—things
like that. Last Saturday we were going to the movies, and I mentioned that I had a headache, and Bill said, well, let's stop at the
drug store and get you some aspirin. Now that may seem like a little
thing, but it was not a little thing for me—no one ever cared about
me enough to do something like that. I feel secure and wanted for
the first time in my life. I have prayed to God many times that I
might one day love and be loved, and Bill seems to be the answer.

Bill says he has prayed about us, too, and he really sincerely
believes that it is God's will for us to marry. I agree. He gave me my
ring tonight—it's a solitaire, not a real big one, but simple and elegant.
I was so happy! And yet when he put it on my finger, it suddenly
looked—how can I explain—kind of like a foreign object, kind of like a
fly in the jam, or something. It was only a momentary feeling, though,
it went away when he held me and told me he loved me.

He is going down to Tulane for medical school next year, and
I already have a teaching job in New Orleans. I will be by his side,
helping him to become the best doctor he can be. I will be a teacher,
yes, but my real job will be supporting Bill in every way I can,
loving him and encouraging him. That is what it means to be a
woman. It's so simple. Loving a man.

CHAPTER 30

in which depression takes control

HEY, SIS, I'M NOT DRUNK! HONEST, I'M NOT. I CAN WALK A STRAIGHT line. Look, watch now, I'm gonna do it.

This is Daddy's "I'm not drunk" routine, running by me one more time. He wobbled across the floor, trying to put one foot in front of the other. I could feel disaster coming on. *Daddy, don't you see I've brought my fiancé home to meet you please, please don't be drunk just this once, I told you we were coming today.*

Daddy, this is Bill Gray. We're going to be married.

What? What did you say, Sis? Daddy reared back on his feet, swaying frontwards and backwards, frontwards and backwards. His green eyes were red and watery from the whiskey, and he began to tear up. Sit down, sit down, he said, and motioned for us to sit, as he groped for one arm of the sofa and eased himself down. *Let's get it over with, Daddy, say your piece. Say your goddamned drunken piece about how much you love me.*

Married, Marilyn? You and this boy? He stared hard at me, and I nodded. He looked at Bill incredulously. I could read his mind. *How could I be getting married? Wasn't I his "pride and joy"? Didn't he still need me?*

Well. Well, well, well, he said. He hung his head over his clasped hands. Tears slipped out and fell on his hands as he tried to take in what I had said. For a while, he said nothing. Then he looked at Bill and said, Well, Son, I want you to take good care of her. That's all I have to say. Just take good care of her.

Now Bill, being the son of a Baptist minister, was not used to people drinking, much less getting drunk, and I could tell he was shaken, because he was dead quiet all the way out of town. Later that night he held me and said he didn't hold my family against me, that it was all right, and he still wanted to marry me.

I didn't believed him, though, couldn't believe him, and the next day when I tried to show off my ring to someone really of no consequence to me, my hand began to shake and I pulled it back and made my escape. It was at that moment that I fell into darkness. A numbness came over me and stayed for a long time.

I felt like a specter, cut off from all living things for days and then weeks and then months. For all this time I was in a separate world. I looked out at others and saw them as objects—there, but unreachable. It was strange, like a waking dream from which I could not awake.

Our wedding date came closer and closer, and I knew I couldn't go through with the ceremony. I called the whole thing off just three weeks before the day I was to become a bride and just before a linen shower my new mother-in-law-to-be was giving so I could meet her friends and receive those basics a bride needs like sheets and towels. I hated to disappoint everyone but knew I shouldn't marry when I felt like killing myself—not that I *would* kill myself, but that's no way to go down the aisle, I knew.

I didn't know what was wrong, or if I'd ever come out of this gloom. I tried to explain to Bill why I couldn't marry him. I asked him, Bill, can you help me, do you know what's happening here? and he said he didn't. His mother told me he was depressed about all this, and I knew that was my fault, but since I couldn't find any remedy for my despair, the wedding was just off. At first I said "postponed," but it was off for good.

I went ahead and moved to New Orleans for my teaching job and Bill went on to medical school at Tulane. We went out a few times, and he kept pushing me to have sex with him because, as he said, he thought he was going to get to have sex and now he couldn't and he had waited a long time. Every time he rubbed my thighs he got so hot he could hardly stand it he said so couldn't we go ahead anyhow. I said no. I was depressed, yes, but I knew I might not always feel that way, and I wanted to be a virgin when I got married. If I lost my virginity now, what would become of me I thought, so I kept saying no, but he just wanted me so bad he said he couldn't think straight, and he said he wouldn't lose respect for me, no, he wouldn't. But I didn't want to risk it.

So we moved away from each other, or rather he moved away from me. I didn't really cry much, I just felt nothing. The depression hung on and hung on, and then after a couple of years, it spontaneously lifted.

🦋

This was the first time a serious depression visited me, though I was to experience depression off and on for the rest of my life. I never once seriously considered suicide, but I can understand why depressed people decide to end their lives. The thing that makes depression unbearable is the isolation. Human creatures get psychic energy from one another, and when we cannot participate in this exchange, we begin to die.

Depressed people know the social script. We smile, because we know we are supposed to. When someone asks, "How are you?" we say "Fine" or even "Great!" After all, we don't want to drag another into our dark world. When we dare to speak the truth to intimates or friends, we see the bewilderment and frustration in their eyes. They want to help, but don't know how. We stop telling people how we feel, lest we become even more isolated.

We know we should get out, try to connect, but anxiety makes us want to move away from the chatter. We go to a concert or a lecture that normally would be of great interest, and we experience nothing. Others around us are talking and laughing in response to the event, and although we hear the words or the music, we simply don't take it in emotionally. We are ever on the periphery, observing. We even observe ourselves observing.

We feel guilty, know we don't measure up, and are convinced that we never will. *Something is wrong with me, and it's never, never going to go away.* Depression is a state more intolerable than any other—more devastating that physical pain, which we understand is a function of the flesh, not of character, or essence. Depression is not the same as grief, which is a normal response to loss, and can offer a cleansing release. Depression is rather a shutting down of the emotive self, a fracturing of the will. It is living behind a glass plate and looking at life on the other side.

We go into the doctor's office, we see a large poster listing "Symptoms of Depression." Seated there on the examining table, surrounded with stainless steel, we read the symptoms while we wait. Oh, we have 7 out of 10. Not a surprise. But we don't bother telling our doctor, because what can he do—just give us some pills? Been there, done that. Suggest that we join a therapy group and talk about ourselves for two hours a week with other people who are depressed? We are convinced that what has taken over our lives won't be touched by pills or talk. So we mention the head-ache. Maybe we have a brain tumor, maybe we can leave this world sooner rather than later, in a more or less respectable way.

We move through the day encased in a bubble, untouched by the life moving all around us. Sadness can be punctured by beauty, grief by hope. But depression disallows the small joys that coax others into wanting to get up another day. We can describe the sunset, but we can't experience the sunset. All the world is barren. We know people care, but no one can reach us. We are outcast, for-saken, a canker sore on the body of the community. We just want the pain to end.

Since individuals on both sides of my family have struggled with mental illness, I believe I have a strong genetic predisposition to depression. Judging from her personality traits, I think my mother was probably bipolar, though her diagnosis was schizophrenia, and she was given shock treatments. She had breakdowns after each of her three children was born, and so must have been susceptible to postpartum depression.

Most of the time my depression is precipitated by a schism in a romantic relationship. I have generally been the one to abandon others, but even so, psychologically I always feel the one abandoned. The tractable fear that I walk with daily becomes a tyrant, without mercy.

My work has been my salvation. Even at my lowest, even during the rare occurrences when thoughts of death plague me for weeks at a time, I can work. Though somewhat impaired, I can write, I can give speeches, I can analyze text, I can lead meetings.

Later on, when counseling and antidepressants became more readily available, I have been fortunate to have a number of excellent doctors who helped me through these difficult times. I continue to encounter depression occasionally, sometimes with quite an overlay of anxiety. My breath grows short, my pulse races. Panic attacks have landed me in the emergency room several times in the past, but not anymore. Generally, I just lie down, breathe deeply, and take the occasional Ativan. Otherwise, I simply accept anxiety as part of my human condition. Everybody has something to deal with, or will have. Depression has been my something.

CHAPTER 31

in which I am saved by the wisdom of an elder

I had broken my engagement, but not before I secured a teaching job in New Orleans, so I was getting ready to make the long drive south when I heard that there was an opening for an English teacher in Claiborne Parish, right there in Homer. Maybe this is what God wants me to do, I thought. I had been feeling guilty about leaving home, anyway. *Maybe this is the way God is speaking to me, telling me through the hurt of losing Bill, that I am supposed to stay at home and take care of the family.* So I phoned the School Board, to get an appointment. I decided to let them speak for God. If it was right for me to stay, I would get the job.

I had an appointment with Mr. Haley, the Superintendent of Schools. I had known his sons Bob and Ben in high school, both good boys—Bob was setting off now to enter medical school, and about ready to marry my friend Brenda. Bob looked for the world like his father—thin, with a head a little too big for his body, and features so sharp that I was always reminded of the plastic life-size human skull sitting on my biology teacher's bookcase, only with a little flesh and skin covering it.

Mr. Haley invited me in, then sat behind his large desk. Not a stray scrap of paper on it. He went right to the heart of our visit: So you want to come back home and teach in Claiborne Parish.

Well, I said, there is an opening, and I thought I would just talk to you and see what you think.

Well you're certainly highly qualified. I have your transcript here—you've distinguished yourself at school, Marilyn. But why do you want to come back here?

Well, my family's here, of course.

And you think you could do them some good if you stayed with them.

Yes, I guess so. I hadn't figured on being found out so soon.

Mr. Haley leaned back in his swivel chair and twirled his thumbs and then twirled his thumbs some more, thinking hard, it seemed to me. His head looked more and more like a skull. *Well, God, now's your chance. If you want me here, you'd better speak up.*

Mr. Haley turned his chair towards me, and put his hands flat on the desk. Marilyn, there's no doubt that you would make a good teacher for us, we could do much worse than hiring you. But I'm not going to hire you. I think you need to leave this town and start your own life apart from your family.

My eyes widened in surprise. *He's decided, just like that?*

Your grandparents are getting up there in years, I know, but they're in good health, they'll be all right. Your father has his problems, but they're his to work out—you can't help him. And your younger brother and sister—they're big enough to manage now without you.

I felt my shoulders relax. I see, I said. Well.

You'll do well wherever you go, Marilyn, but you need to leave Homer.

Yes. Well, thank you, Mr. Haley, for seeing me, I said. I fumbled for my purse, and stood.

He moved from behind his desk and reached out to shake my hand. That's all right. Good luck to you. You'll make us—this town—proud.

Thank you. I really want to thank you, I said. I scurried out the door, wondering at the tears that were rushing to my eyes.

I felt strangely light, the way you do when you take off a heavy coat after walking into a warm room. I smiled to myself all the way home. *I'm supposed to go! I'm not bad for going. Thank you, Mr. Haley. Thank you, God.*

⁂

A friend invited me to attend a lecture at a local hotel one evening several years ago, saying she thought I would be interested in the subject matter. The presenter was Dr. Vincent Felitti, one of the principals in "The Adverse Childhood Experiences Study" done by San Diego Kaiser Permanente. The decade-long study, begun in 1995-97, and since corroborated by several other studies, links ten negative childhood experiences to serious medical conditions and social problems in adulthood, such as depression, obesity, diabetes, heart disease, suicide, drug abuse, poor job performance, unstable relationships. About 17,000 middle-aged adults with Kaiser Permanente health insurance were asked about childhood events and given an ACE (Adverse Childhood Experience) score between 0 and 10, according to whether or not they had experienced a given event. The constellation of these experiences includes growing up in households where there was alcohol abuse; emotional, physical, sexual abuse; emotional or physical neglect; witnessing domestic violence; and growing up with drug abuse, mental illness, parental discord, or crime in the home.

Dr. Felitti flashed chart after chart up into the darkness, showing clearly that *the incidence of these serious problems in adulthood grows in direct proportion to the number of childhood events, or "markers."* I was drawn in, mortified by what I saw. Those individuals who had over 4 markers were highly likely to succumb to serious disease or injury or to suffer from depression or to be heavily addicted to alcohol or drugs. They were likely to experience, in Felitti's words, "premature mortality" (die in their 50's or 60's). At the end of his power-point presentation, Felitti did something startling. He showed us a slide of healthy baby boy, a strawberry blond with an engaging smile—and then he showed us slides of the same child as his physical and emotional health deteriorated through the years: first grade, adolescent, young adult, and then finally scuffy, drug-addled street person with matted red hair and bleary eyes. Felitti said to his rapt audience: "I ask you, how did we get from here (slide of baby) to here (slide of homeless man)?"

I found myself overwhelmed with emotion. Tears spilled out of my eyes, in spite of myself, and I was hoping that Dr. Felitti would not notice, when the lights came up. Why was I crying so uncontrollably? At the time I didn't even know. My painful growing up days were rushing back at me, and I knew that I would never wholly escape them. I had always known that my struggles as an adult were somewhat related to my upbringing—though I had hoped that with each passing year, I would grow stronger and more resilient. And in some ways I had. But the cards in this deck were heavy and way stacked against me, I now understood. I had 7 of the 10 markers. I should be an alcoholic, or in jail, or 100 pounds overweight, or dead. What I was feeling was a rush of primal gratitude.

Yes, I have had to deal with anxiety and depression; yes, intimacy has been difficult for me; yes, my parenting skills were lacking; yes, I am overly controlling with others. But I have not succumbed to obesity, to diabetes, to a heart attack, to mental illness, alcoholism, or drugs. My only addiction has been to work—I have to confess that my life has not been what you call "balanced." But I am one of the lucky ones. I have survived and even flourished, only because many others have cared. It's really that simple. It is true that I have been blessed with an intelligent mind and a curious nature, with physical health, with a reasonably attractive appearance. But all this would have counted for nothing, all this would have not saved me. Only love could have done that.

I thought of my grandparents, who took us three children and their errant son into their home when they were in their 70s, after raising seven children of their own and three others belonging to various relatives.

I thought of our neighbors in Homer, Louisiana, who never

moved the whole time I was growing up, who watched us children from their porches and windows and kept us safe. I thought of Mamie Endom, the next door neighbor who gave me a surprise birthday party when I was 16, the only birthday party I ever had after we left Mother.

I thought of the adults who saw potential in me that I never saw in myself, including my fifth-grade teacher, Mrs. Crump, who wrote on my final report card, "One day I hope to see some of your stories in print." *What could she have meant by that?*

I thought of the high school, where the teachers were invested in the growth and well-being of the students, and where most of the students went off to college, successfully. Mrs. DeSordi, the home economics teacher, taught us girls about menstruation, as well as how to stitch a straight line and how to set the table properly. Miss Holcomb, my senior English teacher, taught me to write a research paper. Mr. Kendall, the band director, taught me to read music. I sang in the chorus directed by Marion Dorman, who had a man's hair cut and wore trousers to school, a flagrantly lesbian woman and talented music teacher who was accepted totally in our small Southern town. I played basketball on the girls' team, and even though our team was not a winning one, I wore my shiny white uniform with gold stripes proudly, and the coach taped my weak ankle before each game.

I thought of the First Baptist Church, where I went Wednesday evening for choir practice and for prayer meeting, and Sunday morning for Sunday school and worship, and Sunday evening for Training Union and church again. I thought of my Sunday school teacher, Miss Altalene, who also worked at White's Dry Goods, and helped me choose fabric to sew skirts and dresses, to take to college. I thought of the Youth Group that met at the church on Sunday night, where we got in a circle and held hands and sang Kum Ba Yah and said sentence prayers from the depths of our young hearts.

I thought of the father who suffered in ways I could never understand as a young girl, a father who in spite of his drinking

and absences loved his three children beyond any doubt whatso-
ever, and managed to pay our way through college by squirreling
away money in the bottom of his cheap chest of drawers.

I thought of Dr. Pat and Dr. James, physicians who knew our
family and came with their black bags to our home when illness
struck any one of us. They followed my grandparents and my father
faithfully through all the years of their lives.

I thought of Louisiana Tech, in Ruston, the first college I attended.
Though I was an English education major, I went to this engineering
school—it was inexpensive and 45 minutes from home. I remember
Dr. Fletcher, a beautiful, soft-spoken English teacher who lost her
fiancé in World War II: she encouraged me to apply for an assistant-
ship to graduate school, my first foray out of North Lousiana.

I thought of Mr. Haley and how he sent me away from home,
when I so desperately needed to leave.

And of course this loving and caring went forward through the
years, through graduate school, through the married years, through
years of struggle during separation and divorce, through preparation
for ministry, through the demanding, exacting profession of ministry.
Various therapists, teachers, doctors, spiritual advisors, churches,
friends—so many, many people have been there for me when I have
needed help. One of my strengths is that when I suffer, I cry out. I
seek help. And I have always found help.

That evening, listening to a researcher in a hotel, with hun-
dreds of others there in the dark—scientists, doctors, social workers,
researchers, many of whom must have been thinking about their own
personal lives, as well as their professions—I came to understand
how very fortunate I am. *Through many dangers, toils and snares, I
have already come.* I understood that everything I have been able to
achieve and anything I can give has been possible only through the
kindness and caring and generosity of others. Now it is my turn to
pass it on, in whatever way I can.

CHAPTER 32

in which I meet the right man

I had been teaching English in New Orleans for four years, the last two at Ben Franklin High School, a public school for gifted children. I loved my work, but was getting lonelier by the day. I knew that I should "get out and meet someone." Everyone said that. *You should go out and meet someone.* The same as if to say, you should go to the corner grocery and get a pound of butter. I had no heart for it. On the other hand, grading papers most nights and on weekends wasn't much of a life. So I made up my mind to try.

I read about a new way for singles to meet—a computer dating service. It may have been the first of its kind anywhere in the United States. The company asked clients to fill out an extensive questionnaire—everything from religious preference to beliefs about sex before marriage. I tried to answer as honestly as I could. That was probably my first mistake, as I was deeply religious and didn't believe in sex before marriage. Anyway, the dating service came with a guarantee, so how could I lose? For my $7.00 fee (not a paltry sum in the '60s), I would receive the names and contact information for at least three men in the New Orleans area who would be compatible with me.

Hopeful, I waited for a response. A month went by, and nothing. Three months, nothing. Six months, still nothing. I was about to give up when I received a message from a computer, written on green graph paper. It was blunt and unequivocal: "There is no one in the New Orleans area who is compatible with you." Just as I thought! And I didn't even get a refund of my $7.00 fee.

For want of a better alternative, I started attending a book discussion group at the Presbyterian Church coffee house just off St. Charles, near my apartment on Fifth Street. Week after week, every Friday night, the same four of us gathered around the battered wooden table upstairs in the church hall: the minister's wife, shy and sweet; the Cornell graduate, an articulate young woman who had started the group; the youngish non-descript man who was mostly quiet; and me.

One evening the group was discussing *The Feminine Mystique*, by Betty Friedan. The book spoke to me—I found so many of my own thoughts and feelings staring back at me in print. Just about the time the discussion was winding down, we heard footsteps on the stairs. A tentative voice asked, Is this where the book discussion is? It was a distinctly Southern voice, and male. And then a man appeared at the top of the stairs, a young man with curly salt and pepper hair and thick glasses, which he adjusted upward on his nose.

This is where it *was*, I answered. We're just finishing.

I saw your sign at Charity Hospital, he said. About the book discussion.

I sat up straighter in my chair. Do you work there?

Yes. I'm a surgery resident.

Sit down, I said. You're at the right place.

So eager was our fledgling group to have a potential new member that we carried on the discussion for another forty-five minutes. I noticed that the new fellow—Frank was his name—seemed totally unthreatened by the ideas in Friedan's book. He didn't say much at all, but seemed accepting of everybody else's remarks. I wanted to find out more about him. After the meeting, I lingered outside on the sidewalk hoping that he would want to talk. I was not disappointed.

Well, well. That's a good group, he said, his hands in his pockets.

We've been meeting for two or three months now, I said.

Well. Where would you be from, with an accent like that? Texas?

No. Louisiana. Not New Orleans—North Louisiana. I just moved down here to teach. Near Texas, though. Do you know where Shreveport is? I'm from a small town near there.

He adjusted his glasses again and began jingling the change in his pockets. Where are you from? I asked him. Somewhere in the South. Tennessee?

No, Kentucky. The Blue Grass. A small town near Lexington. The jingling grew louder, and his pockets were alive with the movement. How about if we—would you like to go get a cup of coffee sometime?

I gave him my phone number, and I had to wait only a few days for the phone call, a call I was sure would come.

Hello, Marilyn? This is Frank. I'm the . . .

I remember, I said. Yes. The doctor. I'm glad you called.

We went to a movie, arriving late because he couldn't get away from the hospital—the beginning of a pattern, I was to learn. The name of the film escapes me, but as I remember, it involved of a lot of WW I airplanes dueling in the skies. After a half hour of this, I told Frank that I hated war movies and was going into the foyer to wait for him until the film was over. Befuddled, he came looking for me, and we went somewhere where we could talk.

I quizzed him. So you're a surgeon?

Well, I'm a resident. I have four years to go in the program before I'll actually be a surgeon.

So you're a doctor now, and you'll be a surgeon.

Yes.

Are you a good doctor? I asked.

Frank smiled and paused. I'm not a great doctor, he said. And I'm not a bad doctor.

So you're a *mediocre* doctor? I asked, smiling. I liked his humility and sense of balance.

He laughed. I'm just an ordinary doctor, I suppose. I like my work. My dad's a doctor, too, so I grew up knowing that I would be a doctor like him.

He was intelligent and well brought up, I thought. Maybe this was the man I had been waiting for. I knew by his pleated pants and his Volkswagen squareback that if he ever chose me, he would never think to leave.

CHAPTER 33

in which my life is endangered

ON OUR SECOND DATE, FRANK TOOK ME TO DINNER AT DELMONICO'S, ON St. Charles Avenue, one of the finest restaurants in the city, a place where a man takes a woman when he wants to impress her—and I have to admit, I was impressed. Unfortunately, that was the evening there was a shoot-out at the restaurant.

Delmonico's was fairly crowded, mainly with older, wealthier couples, dressed elegantly. The lights were low, but not too low, the tables far enough apart to allow intimacy. Frank and I were eating our salads and having polite conversation when suddenly shots rang out. Pow-pow, pow-pow!

I knew what a gun sounded like—after all, I was from the South where men hunt and where guns hang on the wall—so I yelled, Hit the floor, that's gunfire!

More gunfire ensued: pow-pow, pow-pow-pow! Everyone in the restaurant got on the floor, including a number of corpulent women in evening dress, their heads down, their rear ends in the air. Everyone except Frank, that is. Frank continued to sit upright, eating his salad. I was crouched on the floor, pulling on his pants leg, begging him, please please get down, but all to no effect.

Those were only fireworks, he said. Don't be silly. Get up from there. He was clearly embarrassed by my behavior.

The shooting stopped, and an ominous silence hung in the air for about thirty seconds before the maître d' appeared. He uttered the classic phrase you always hope you'll never hear: Is there a doctor in the house? Frank looked around slowly and gingerly raised his hand.

It appears that a chauffeur of one of the diners had gone berserk and started waving a gun at a passing police car. If you know anything at all about New Orleans, you know you can be killed by the police for considerably less than that. The policemen called in recruits, and soon a whole bevy of police were shooting it out with the chauffeur. The chauffeur was shot through the heart who knows how many times and was quite dead. A policeman was seriously injured, and another had a superficial bullet wound that sliced him just over the ear. Frank rode with the ambulance to take the two policemen to the hospital, and I went home alone in a taxi. A doctor goes when he's called. I was beginning to learn what it might be like to be married to a surgeon.

❧

On our third date Frank took me sailing. I had never been sailing. I thought, How romantic! I made a special lunch featuring stuffed artichokes. We drove out to Lake Ponchartrain and stopped on the shore, but I saw no marina, no sailboats. As it turned out, our boat was in three canvas bags in the back of Frank's Volkswagen squareback. I watched while he assembled it.

We launched the little craft just fine, but we didn't get far—the mast got stuck under the causeway. Frank began paddling furiously to get us unstuck, and suddenly I noticed a billfold floating in the water.

Is that your billfold? I asked.

Be quiet, just keep paddling! he ordered. But a moment later he slapped his back pocket and shouted, That *is* my billfold, and I just got paid! The billfold was beginning a slow descent to the bottom of the lake, and Frank jumped in after it—too late. Just then the mast came unstuck. A gust of wind grabbed the boat, moving it quickly across the waves, with me the only sailor. We had no life jackets. At first, Frank tried to swim for the boat. But it was clear that it was moving way too fast for him to catch it, so he reversed himself and swam for the causeway. He swam frantically, swam for his life, as I watched helplessly. He went down three times, and I began thinking how ironic it would be for someone with all that education to drown in a stupid accident.

In the meantime, the wind was taking me swiftly out to the middle of Lake Ponchartrain. I managed to take down the sail, but as I was standing upright, with huge waves slapping at the fragile little craft, it occurred to me that if I fell out, I was dead. Sobered, I sat down and clenched the side of the boat. Dusk was falling, and I had no light to signal anyone. I knew that if I could just stay with the boat, I would be found at some point—but when?

Then out of the night, I saw a light moving towards the boat—it was the Coast Guard. Strong arms lifted me safely on board, and then the men put Frank's boat on their boat. They took me back to the Coast Guard station, where I was reunited with Frank. He had been lucky enough to swim to a ladder leading up to the freeway—there was one every four miles along the bridge—and the state police had picked him up. No one else would, because he was covered with vomit. I found him with a blanket over his shoulders, soaking his feet in a tub of hot water, and shivering. He was just glad to be alive. Me, too.

CHAPTER 34

in which I decide to marry

LET'S GET MARRIED, FRANK WOULD SAY.

I don't know. I just don't think you love me. I just don't know, I would respond.

I love you, Poo. That was his nickname for me—Poo, without the *h*.

But I don't *feel* like you love me.

Let's get married.

Frank just kept being there and kept saying, Let's get married. After three years of dating him, I took stock. In those days if a woman was not married at twenty-five, she was on the verge of being called an old maid. I was twenty-eight. I couldn't see much ahead for me without Frank. Without anyone. So I said yes to him, told him at the airport just before he flew back to Kentucky to his Granddaddy Madison's funeral.

Let's do it soon, I said.

Frank seemed happy, at least as happy as he ever seemed. His mood was always steady, neither high nor low. When he got back Sunday night, he said he told his family that we were going to get married, and said how glad everybody was. We had been going together plenty long enough, and Frank was thirty-two, so the family figured it was about time we got on with it.

We drove back to my place and talked about the wedding. It would be in three months, no use delaying things. We would be married right here in New Orleans, where our friends lived. We stayed up until 2:00 a.m. talking and planning.

Come on into the bedroom, and hold me, Frank, I said, and he did, and we were soon under the covers, and soon had our clothing off, and were lying close, kissing and touching. I thought that maybe we would make love that night, which I didn't believe in doing before marriage, although that night was different, because we were engaged. But he thought we ought to wait. I wanted to respect his convictions, so I didn't question anything. I fell asleep with his arms around me.

The next thing I knew, the sun was rising, and I was beginning to wake up. I blinked and blinked again. There was Frank, on the pillow next to mine, sleeping soundly. He had stayed through the night! I stared at him, and smiled. He looked even more innocent when he was sleeping. A great wave of warmth moved through me. I knew that he would never abandon me. *I hope I can learn to love you, Frank, I hope I'm a good wife, and I never hurt you.*

Frank stirred. He opened his eyes slowly and looked at me. You're here, he said, and reached for me.

Yes, I answered, kissing him gently on the cheek. I'm here. I'm not going away.

CHAPTER 35

in which I do what a girl must do

I SET IT UP THE WAY I THOUGHT A WEDDING OUGHT TO BE: A MODEST ceremony in a little chapel borrowed from the Methodists, charming, with brilliant stained-glass windows all around, including one of Jesus as a shepherd. I sent out formal invitations with my father's name to friends and family. I found a dressmaker to create a Victorian-looking wedding dress with puff sleeves and a high neckband, upon which I pinned a cameo I found in the French Quarter and bought for myself.

I carried a multi-colored spring bouquet, had two bridesmaids, and for the reception, ordered a three-tiered cake with a bride and groom on top. I was still a virgin, more or less, at age twenty-eight. I wanted to do everything right. I hired a photographer so that I could make it real and remember it all and have a regular album, the way you are supposed to, when you're in love and you get married.

My fear grew as my wedding day approached—I realized that my father was a potential problem. He was always drunk on special occasions. I wondered if I should invite him at all. Maybe he would ruin the whole event. I didn't want him to walk me down the aisle and "give me away." I did not belong to him. But of course I *did* belong to him—he was my father. So in the end I did ask him to give me away, because that was the part he was supposed to play.

I got Uncle Lemos, Daddy's youngest brother, to watch him and not let him near any alcohol on the day of the wedding. So when the time came, I took my father's arm, and we got down the aisle just fine. The pictures show a strange, forelorn look on his face, though. You would think he had a broken heart.

Everything went as planned. About eighty people were there—my Louisiana relatives and the friends I had made at school and at church in New Orleans. I asked the minister to include that passage from Ruth, "Entreat me not to leave thee, or to return from following after thee: For wither thou goest, I will go; and where thou lodgest, I will lodge. . . ."

After the reception, I changed into my beige going-away suit with matching shoes and pillbox hat, and threw the multi-colored bouquet from the church steps. Frank and I had only one day for a honeymoon before he had to be back at the hospital, so we just drove down to the Royal Sonesta, a fancy hotel in the French Quarter, to spend our wedding night.

That night I made love for the very first time. It was altogether more ordinary than I imagined it might be, and messier. The important thing was that I was married, though. I had become Mrs. Frank Sewell, Jr. I had a home of my own and a man who would never leave me.

CHAPTER 36

in which I learn the nature of love

NO SOONER THAN WE MARRIED WE MOVED TO LIVERPOOL, ENGLAND, where Frank began a pediatric surgery residency at Alder Hey Hospital. Having left my friends and a teaching job I loved, only to find myself in a strange world where language itself was sometimes indecipherable, I began sliding into depression.

I was sitting in a dentist chair one day, and when the dentist greeted me with a casual How are you? I found myself saying that I was thinking about killing myself. Not that I would. But he took my words seriously and walked me across the medical campus to a psychiatrist's office. To my surprise, the doctor did not want to hear about my childhood. He gave me a prescription for an anti-depressant, and in several weeks, my mood miraculously lifted. I decided that I wanted to have a baby. It was time. I got pregnant on the first try.

I knew I was beautiful, my belly being swollen with the child. Eyes fell on me wherever I went and the eyes said there's something growing there, something new coming, and we have a stake in it, this new thing. In a way I was doing it for them all, I was God's breath blowing over them all. At least, that's how I felt.

My gynecologist didn't understand the sacred nature of the enterprise. On my initial visit, I was stripped and up on a table, and the first words out of his mouth were "spread your legs." I thought a different phrase would have been better suited for the occasion. But then some people wouldn't know the Angel Gabriel himself if he flew down and sat on their dinner plate.

The pregnancy wasn't any trouble at all. It was the usual trouble, of course, like weird cravings, a sore back, and trouble sleeping because of having to get up and run to the bathroom, but not really trouble the way you think of trouble as something you don't want or can't bear. It was the kind of trouble you have when you do any kind of making—you give yourself to it and don't care that you missed your lunch or that your jeans got dirty, because it's all a gift to the making. As for me, I smiled nearly all the time during my pregnancy. Smiling like that was so out of the ordinary for me that my smile muscles got tired and started aching. Can you imagine your biggest problem being that you smile all the time? That's the way it was for me, being pregnant with Kash.

The doctor said he had a lecture to give in Rochester the day after the baby was supposed to come, so if my labor was late, he was going to induce me, which I didn't want. It seemed to me that the baby would know best when he's ready to come out and deal with this world.

It turned out that Kash was one jump ahead of the doctor, and on the very evening before my due date, I went into labor. Frank took me out for Chinese food. He said it was going to be a while before the baby came.

He drove me to the hospital and left me with the nurses for the "prep," while he made rounds. I hated being shaved like that—it was such a foreign experience—and I began to feel frightened and forlorn. I felt the pain slipping in and then subsiding, and I understood more surely than before that my body was not my own, that I could in no way control this unfolding to come and that my flesh would break and bleed. When Frank came back, I asked, Are you going to be with me tonight?

It'll be twelve to twenty-four hours before the baby comes, he said. I need to go home and get some rest. I've got surgery tomorrow.

No, I wanted to say, You're my husband and I need you with me. But I couldn't say it. It never even occurred to me to say it.

OK, I said. And I told myself that I was fine with his going. But at that very moment another thought arose, unbidden—*that's all right, the baby and I can do this alone, I don't need you.* We'll be all right, I said. And he left. But with that encounter, a division came between us, a shadow dropped, and healing never completely came.

Do you want anything for pain? the nurse asked. I wasn't hurting much. So I told her, No.

By the next afternoon, though, the contractions got heavier and heavier and closer together, no stopping them, any more than the waves of the oceans. I just let the pains sweep over me, again and again and again, and I gave myself to the inevitability of it, the hurt and all, owning it, taking it all in. Toward the end my doctor gave me the epidural he had promised, so I was awake and could push. After a good hour and half's work, Kash slipped out. You've got yourself a boy, said the doctor. And a big one. Congratulations.

Frank had been waiting outside while I was in the delivery room—after all, he had said, you wouldn't want another doctor looking over your shoulder if something goes wrong while you're trying to deliver his baby, would you? And I said I understood.

Everybody's different, you just have to take people like they are, I reasoned, and Frank was who he was. Right after the birth he came in and examined Kash to be sure the baby was perfect. After he had looked him over top to toe and was satisfied, he left to phone family and to drink champagne with his doctor friends.

Kash and I, we didn't need anybody, we celebrated together, he trying out his new little lungs, crying for upwards of an hour and I, just floating on my back on that table, as though adrift on the ocean of being, my torn and bleeding body full of praise, full of grace. Amen.

CHAPTER 37

in which I remember my mother's love

WHEN FRANK AND I RETURNED TO THE STATES WITH OUR INFANT SON, WE settled in Lexington, Kentucky, near his parents in Mt. Sterling. I was pregnant with our second child.

At that point, I knew my mother mostly through her letters and angry phone calls to Louisiana, as my memory of my life with her had been wiped almost clean. It was as if I were dead to those early years of childhood. But now came this new opportunity, for Lexington was a mere eighty miles from Cincinnati, where she still lived, in an apartment owned by her brother Buddy. Not that I wanted to get to know her—I didn't. But I knew I should try. She had contracted breast cancer while we were in Liverpool, and I didn't know how much longer she would live. She had a right to know her grandchildren. And she wanted to be with me, to have a relationship of whatever kind with her eldest child before she died. She believed that God had sent me back to her, she said.

So every month or so I drove the red Volvo the eighty miles to Cincinnati and stayed with Mother for a few hours. Having had a beer or two, or more, to counter her nerves, she would be waiting expectantly, her dark eyes shining. She would bring out bowls of treats for the boys—all the stuff that I never let them eat at home, like potato chips and M&M's. They loved these snacks, of course, and they welcomed their grandmother's eager hugs and kisses. Laughter filled the small apartment.

But for me my mother was still a stranger. I was raised in the

South, where women were brought up to be delicate and soft-spoken. Mother's voice tended to be loud and, after a drink or two, raucous. Her hands were rough and cold. Or maybe it was my heart that was cold.

Who was this woman who had birthed me? If I came from her body, how could we be so different?

From time to time, she was hospitalized with yet another surgery, and I visited her in the hospital. I hardly knew what to do, what to say. On one such visit, I asked her if she wanted me to brush her hair—it had just been washed that morning and was still just barely damp, fragrant from the shampoo, and tangled. She could sit up, the nurse said, it was all right, so I helped her to a chair. She moved like a wounded creature, tender of herself, and slow, and she sat with a heaviness I had not seen in her previously, as though her veins were running lead instead of good red blood and she was carrying a load, just to stay alive and breathe and move. But if I asked her how she was, she would say fine or good every time.

※

I take the ebony hair brush she had brought from home, the fine old one with the stiff brown bristles now grown soft that she's used from before I can remember, and I stand behind her and begin to brush her hair back from her face and towards me, her head responding to the pressure of the brush, each stroke pulling her closer to me. She seems to like it, and makes little grunting sounds, like small children make when they're about to fall asleep, tired out from play and unable to hold their eyes open another minute. I brush with my strong right hand, and my left is all the while smoothing the hair back on her forehead, the side of her face, her neck beneath the hairline. I look at the pattern of gray, the widow's peak in front, widening out to a larger streak towards the back. It looks like a path through a trackless woods. She keeps saying how good it feels, so I keep brushing and brushing, the dark strands in my hand, pulling her close. It is all I know to do.

Marilyn, will you be still—the reason it hurts is that you keep wriggling while I'm trying to brush it. Just relax, Honey, and let me do it.

Mother is brushing my hair hurriedly, impatiently, this morning. Braids take time, and she is afraid I will be late for school. I'm sitting upright in the chair in front of her dresser, trying not to move. The brushing takes on a rhythm, the bristles of the brush don't hurt unless I resist, and my scalp tingles with pleasure.

Mommy, where is God? Mother is startled by the question. She is not ready to discuss theology so early in the morning, and nothing in her Catholicism has prepared her for the questions of a six-year-old. The Catechism says "omnipresent," but that will not do it. She frowns, she brushes a bit harder.

God is everywhere, she says at last.

Is God in that bug? I ask, pointing to a betsy bug laboring its way across the top of the dresser.

Well, uh, yes, I guess He is, she answers. Everywhere includes bugs.

Do you know God? I ask.

Quick tears spring to her eyes, and she is not sure why. She questions herself, realizing that she wants to know God, but wonders whether in fact she does know God at all. She goes to Mass daily. She prays her rosary. But does she know God? She is full of anger, full of tears at times, because her husband, whom she loves beyond measure, is seeing another woman. When he comes home, he comes with whiskey on his breath. She says nothing to me, for she does not know what to say and she does not want to say the wrong thing. She is empty of meaning, and full of wanting.

Well, do you, Mommy? I persist.

She divides the long strands of hair and begins the braiding. Do you know how Mommy holds you at night and sings to you before you go to sleep?

Yes, I say and nod. It is my favorite time of the day. With Mother, in the rocking chair.

Keep your head still now, Honey. Well, God holds you all the time, just like that. He holds all of us. But we sometimes forget that God's arms are there, we get so busy or so worried. Sometimes even Mommy forgets. But God never goes away. God loves us all the time. Mother stops her braiding and wipes her eyes and takes my head in her hands and bends over and kisses me on the forehead. God is always with you, she says.

⁂

I finish my brushing and she begins nodding off, so I say to her, wouldn't you like to crawl back into bed and take a nap and I'll come back and see you tonight, and she says yes, that might be best, I'll get a little nap before they bring in my dinner. She eases back into her sheets—she isn't quite with me anymore, I know, and as I cover her and kiss her pale cheek, her eyes close. She is almost gone, a half-smile on her mouth, the black hair a wreath around her head there on the white pillow.

CHAPTER 38

in which a memory returns

I once had long hair, honey-blond, curling softly down to my waist. That was before my friend Susan got a pageboy. I thought she was beautiful, and I wanted to be beautiful in the same way. So I begged my mother, pleaded with her until she was sick of hearing about it. Please let me get my hair cut, Mother. Please. *Please*.

Mother said I would be sorry if I did. It would take years and years to grow out again, she warned. But I insisted, wouldn't let up day and night, and so she finally agreed. If that's what you want, you can do it, she said. But you won't like it, mark my words.

All the while my picture of Susan was before me, the way the line of hair curved round her cheek, accenting her high cheekbones. When she moved, her straight bob shifted and caressed her face. When she was still, it made a lovely frame for her perfect skin and violet eyes.

I sat before the big mirror, the white cape tied round my neck, the lights glaring down. Hardly daring to breathe, I waited for transformation. The hairdresser cut the length off with one swoop around my head. She lay the mass of hair in my lap, and began trimming and shaping. Snip, snip. Snip, snip. Still no Susan emerged. More trimming. No Susan. My nose was too long for this new style, I saw at once. And my hair curled even more insistently, now that it was short. Instead of lying flat at the sides, it stuck out, in stubborn waves and curls. I looked like a poodle with a bad trim.

As I stared into the mirror, big tears pushed their way out of my eyes, though I made no sound. The hairdresser wrapped the hank of hair in a large piece of tissue paper, and handed it to me. Well, I think it's as cute as it can be, Honey, she said. It'll take a while to get used to, that's all.

I continued to cry. I cried all the way home, all through dinner (which I didn't eat), and all through that evening. It was time for bed, and I was still crying. Mother came in and sat on my bed. It'll grow back, Sweetheart. In no time at all. You'll see. She stroked my forehead again and again. She held my hand. Oh, Honey. It's going to be all right. You'll see. Her perfume made it seem like a promise. Finally I dropped off to sleep, sniffling still.

It never grew back, of course. I kept the hank of hair in my bedside drawer. Not long after that, Daddy took us South. Daddy said I could take only a few clothes, but I hid the hair underneath. I kept it in a cardboard box in the back bedroom, where Daddy slept, along with the five-year diaries I filled and my drawings. Later I included the articles I wrote for the school newspaper, and my yearbooks. The hair stayed blonde, as I grew dark and tall.

The years went by, and I forgot about the coil of hair most of the time. But sometimes on rainy days when I had nothing to do and a long emptiness seemed to settle in, I went to my special box and sifted through the contents. The paper was going limp and had that sweet smell of loss and decay. Whenever I went there, I saw a blonde curl peeking out the bottom of the tissue in which I kept the hair. I would unwrap the coil and look at the length of it.

Could I have ever been this blonde? When had the darkness come? This could have been the hair of an angel. Surely it was not mine. But here was the proof of what once was. I felt my mother's hands braiding my hair. I heard her voice, Hold still now, or else it'll hurt. I held still, and it hurt anyway. She comforted me, It'll be all right, Sweetheart. You'll see.

When Granny and Big Papa died, within six months of each other—I came home for both their funerals, of course—it didn't occur to me to get my store of special things. I guess I thought my box would be there in the house forever, but that's not the way it happens after people die. Other people go through their belongings and throw out most everything, because one person's memories are another person's trash.

So I couldn't really blame my aunts and uncles for throwing the stuff out—though you would think that they would understand at least that the yearbooks were important, and the awards, but they didn't. It all got pitched, including the hank of hair. Maybe it was kind of strange, anyway, keeping the hair all that time, I thought, but when I found out it was gone, I was sad. I was sad for days. I was sad about the yearbooks and the drawings and the articles, too, but not as sad as I was about the hair. My blond angel hair. Gone who knows where.

CHAPTER 39

in which I search, once again, for Mother

I RECENTLY RECEIVED WHAT WAS LEFT OF MY MOTHER'S SCRAPBOOK FROM my cousin Geri, who grew up in Cincinnati and knew my mother well. When I looked inside, I found a dusty plastic bag containing shards of my mother's early life on the stage. I sifted through the yellowed, crumbling pages, examining the photos, the letters, poems, news articles and memorabilia. I moved carefully through the scrapbook, because at every touch, more of each page fell to pieces, wafting out of my hands.

I saw pictures of people she loved, but I never knew; articles about people she admired, but whom I had never heard of; ads from clubs she attended; playbills and pictures from venues where she danced; a greyhound bus ticket that took her home to Cincinnati; a column by Walter Winchell; a ticket to a golf exhibition at the Belle Haven Country Club, Sunday, May 26, 1935, admission fifty cents; a card with a dim fingerprint in a box, from J. Edgar Hoover, Director of the Federal Bureau of Investigation; a business card of her own: **_Geo. P. Gross Studio of Dance, under direction of Miss Marion Denton_** ("Marion Denton" was her stage name); a program from the annual Goody convention held at the St. Moritz Hotel in New York; a written message, scratched out on a piece of stationery, and carefully preserved: "Just a tiny gift to Marion from the one person who would like to give her the whole world. I love you."

Could this have been from my father? No, of course not—he would not have known her then. She was so fully alive, brimming with romance and passion: other men would have been in love with her, too.

On the back of most pages, Mother wrote her impressions of people and places, all remote references for me, but I marveled—at one time this was her life. Some of the writing is illegible, and parts of sentences are missing because of the condition of the album, but even what is clearly legible doesn't necessarily cohere. A typical entry reads: Raleigh Habadashery Shop—New England Restaurant—Gin Rickey—the best in Washington—the Jewish boy—who could have been a brother of Ken Wise—his theme song "Stay as Sweet as You Are"—the trip to Norfolk called off . . .

What could all these bits have had in common? Only she knew.

Many of her references hinted at flirtations with men: George McDonough—the New York Play Boy—the perfect wit . . . 6 ft 4—Jack Kelly—Grand dancer—Roast pork dinner—A most pleasant day but disappointing—Au Revoir! Don—Formerly in show business—cute trick of an Irishman. Douglas—"If I had on pajamas blue/ And I was cuddled close to you/ Would you? . . . kiss me?"

Apparently a lot of sentimental poetry was published in newspapers during that era, and these kinds of poems filled pages of her scrapbook, typical themes dwelling upon faith, patience, courage, and hope—qualities that were perhaps especially coveted by a young woman trying to make it on her own as a dancer during the Great Depression.

Toward the end of my searching, I found a large picture of a baby, with tousled blonde hair, sitting in her high chair, laughing. Underneath the picture Mother had written the following words:

I am so sure I have forgotten you—
Until—by chance within a crowd I see—
A smile that captures as yours used to do—
And find I still am <in> thrall to memory—
I am so sure—until I hear one day—
A tone of voice, in spite of all the sages say—

I know that neither time nor space insures
Against remembering. I also know
This exquisite encounter with old pain
Is something that my heart would not forego . . .

And the rest is missing, has fallen off the edge. I have to fill in the blanks myself. The tears come. I ask myself why I'm so moved by this really bad poetry. I wonder if she wrote this herself. Was she thinking of me? Or maybe of my sister, or maybe of all three of her missing children? But wait—this album was created before she met my father. Did she somehow know what lay in store? What deep memories was she living with? Was my flesh even then connected to hers? "I know that neither time nor space insures/ Against remembering."

I have carried a kind of nameless fear inside me all of my days. People tell me I am "self-contained," "strong," "independent," but the truth is, I grew up being absolutely convinced that I was different, that there was something about me, some essence that was profoundly flawed, spoiled at birth—no, from conception itself—something so basic it could not be redeemed, something that rendered me inherently unlovable. Some would blame St. Augustine and original sin for this deep-seated self-doubt—and perhaps more than anyone else, he was responsible for the guilty wash coloring all of Western culture. As for me, I think I missed my mother's arms.

The ever-present problem for a grown-up who was not attended to as a child is that the adult has no gauge for discernment in relationship. *Am I asking too much? Am I asking too little? Am I right in feeling hurt, or I'm just being overly sensitive?* So it has been hard for me to know what I could rightly expect from others. It becomes difficult even to recognize and acknowledge preference and desire.

Do you like me? Could you love me?

If your mother doesn't want you, then who would want you? The child's psyche is primitive, and makes its mark deep.

So this "strong and independent" woman looks for caretakers of various kinds: doctors, psychotherapists, breathing teachers, spiritual directors, masseuses, house cleaners, gardeners—whoever will come, whoever will care. I can just make an appointment, and then write a check. Their service is predictable, and clear professional limitations insure that these arrangements do not carry the danger of rejection or betrayal. I don't have to guess whether or not they will be there for me. I pay them to care.

CHAPTER 40

in which I learn the power of story

I'VE NOTICED THAT I CAN FALL INTO STUCK PLACES THAT WILL NOT LET ME go for a long time. At those times, I feel like an insect caught in a web, squirming and straining, to no avail. I suffer. I complain. Sometimes I fall into despair. Then there is a flurry of angel wings, my own little annunciation. New life starts.

As the wife of a surgeon, my job was that of making a home: supporting my husband, caring for our two young sons, and seeing that the house was orderly and food on the table. I did not work outside the home—in that time and in that place, doctor's wives did not work. We lived in an historic section of town, in a restored Victorian with six carved fireplaces and tall stained glass windows. I loved the house—its extraordinary beauty and spaciousness fed my soul. I was financially secure, I had a maid, a nanny from England for the children, and friends at Central Baptist, where we attended. On the surface of things, my life was one to be envied.

But I began having mysterious headaches, which the doctor said were psychosomatic, and so he sent me to group therapy. The group encouraged me to reveal my feelings. First I had to recognize my feelings, of course, and I wasn't sure how to do that. I had a lot to learn.

What I did know is that my brain was turning to mush from disuse. I needed to get out of the house, to engage the larger world in some way. So I signed up for a creative writing course with Wendell Berry, a poet, novelist, and essayist who was teaching at the University of Kentucky and was just becoming well known at the time. I had never met him, though, and was unprepared for the power of our first encounter.

When I entered class that first day, the students were gathering around a circular table. I plunked myself down just to the left of Wendell, and that was to be my place thereafter. Wendell was tall and lean and had the hard muscular build and the hands of a workingman. I soon discovered that he was a farmer as well as a writer and a teacher.

On that first day Wendell read to us from *Paradise Lost* and then read a short story by his friend Gurney Norman, an initiation story set in Eastern Kentucky. I was moved by this teacher, and I didn't quite know why. His voice was soft, all Kentucky, but he spoke out of some deep place within himself, from some place of integrity and purpose. When he laughed, that came from the depths of him, too. *Here is a man whose life is given over.* I knew that I must be with him for a while and learn what I could learn.

Our first assignment was to write a story and bring it to the next class. I had written for a number of years, and had published a few pieces, but always articles and book reviews, never fiction. I was not a fiction writer, I knew. I wondered what I could write about. I decided arbitrarily, to write an essay on the subject of examinations. And why not? I had been examined by teachers throughout my long academic career, and I had rarely found such evaluation useful. I knew I had a way with words. I was confident that my long essay was well written—carefully reasoned, well constructed, graceful, and perfectly punctuated.

Wendell returned our papers at the end of the next class meeting. I could hardly believe his response—there was no grade, just a blanket rejection. He had written, Where is your authority to make these statements? Give me something of yourself.

The other students filed out, many no doubt similarly disappointed in Wendell's response to their work, but I stood there as if my feet were screwed into the floor, clutching my paper and staring, unable to stifle the huge tears rolling down my face. *What did he mean, give me something of yourself?* All I could say was, I don't know what to do. I don't know what to do.

Wendell shifted from one foot to the other and blinked his eyes in discomfort—he hadn't intended to hurt me. Come and see me, he said, and we'll talk.

Wendell kept sending my papers back, all that semester. No comments at all. I knew that he was asking for more from me and that he was right, but I could not articulate the change. I wrote feature stories for the local newspaper, stories like "The Making of a Draft Resister" and "Female Volunteerism Easier in South America." I reviewed Wendell's new book, *The Memory of Old Jack.* I went regularly to Wendell's office and talked about my work. And I talked about my life. Every time I went, some tenderness in me felt exposed.

There was something about Wendell's presence that called for truth-telling. He listened and he listened, mostly with his long legs propped up on his desk. He laughed. He asked pointed questions. He said what he thought about my responses. One day he invited me to his farm: Why don't you come to the farm and see Tanya and me, he said. I told him I would have to check with my husband, check his schedule, and Wendell said, Why don't you just come alone. I began to think I was worth something. I kept writing.

All during my academic career in college and graduate school, I was the quintessential straight-A student. My other teachers had all told me how good I was. Wendell was the only one who asked me for more. And he was the only one who taught me anything about writing. Tell the truth about what you know, he said. That's all.

But telling the truth was the most difficult thing in the world, I thought. I was beginning to understand what that kind of honesty means for a writer: the choice of a single word can reveal an old desperation still alive; a metaphor which takes you unaware can awaken you, can quite literally change the pattern of your life.

I began work on a personal essay late in the semester. The final day of class came too soon. I had been up all night in a last-ditch effort to finish my essay, something that would be from myself, something that would be honest. I was still typing my paper at 7:30 a.m., when Kash wandered downstairs for his morning hug, and breakfast. With him on my lap, I typed the ending of the piece on my old Remington Rand portable, the one my father had given me for high school graduation. It was that or a mutton coat, he said. I chose the typewriter.

I heard the waking-up sounds of my younger son, Madison, and went upstairs to change him and bring him down for breakfast. Amidst the milk and bananas and cereal, I finished the paper. There was no time for proofreading. My class was at nine, and I rushed to get dressed, but at 8:40 the babysitter had still not shown up. What could I do? I was suddenly struck with the clear necessity to go to class. Nothing in my life had ever been clearer. *I will be in class today.*

It was December, and snow was on the ground. I quickly bundled up the boys in their snowsuits, put them in the back seat of the station wagon, and raced off for the hospital, where Frank had gone earlier that morning to do surgery. I parked in the emergency room parking lot and took Kash and Madison on the elevator up to the fourth floor, to the surgery department. I said to the receptionist, Here are Dr. Sewell's two children. He'll have to look after them this morning. I kissed the children goodbye and left before the open-mouthed young woman could regain her composure.

Class began in the usual fashion that morning, Wendell asking if anyone was prepared to read. He looked to his left, where I was scrunched down, trying to hide from his gaze. I demurred, saying only that I had a piece I *could* read, if nobody else had anything. Wendell then went all the way around the circle, asking each in turn, but it was final exam time, and no one had anything to read that day. So he said, Well, then, let's begin again. Marilyn, do you have anything to read?

I tentatively agreed to read, and the floor was mine by default. I had no sense of whether or not my essay was any good. I knew only that I had at last tried my best to be honest in a piece of writing.

I began reading about my severe depression after the breaking of my first engagement, about friends who tried to help but couldn't, about a husband who loved me from a distance, about my troubles teaching little English boys in Liverpool and my tenacious love for those students, and finally about my first pregnancy and giving birth. As I read, I began to cry, and I continued to cry all the way through the reading of the nineteen pages, not once raising my eyes. When I finished, I threw the paper at Wendell—half in spite, half in triumph—and said, Here, that's what you wanted.

After a long silence, I looked up uneasily to see how members of the class were reacting. To my surprise, many of them were crying, too. There was not the usual period of analysis and criticism—rather, after a few quiet moments, people said goodbye to one another, and each had a warm word or a hug for me. I had touched these individuals, it occurred to me, by simply revealing who I was. They were drawn to me, not because I was confident, strong, intelligent, superior—the way I had always tried to present myself—but because I was honest about myself: I was mean, generous, naive, confused, hopeful, determined, angry, and loving. I was all of these contradictions and more—and all that I was, was acceptable.

When the others had all gone, I looked at Wendell. He was standing there, his long bony frame seeming more awkward and boyish than usual. He was holding my paper in his hands. Tears had stolen into his eyes. He said, Now don't you let yourself think of this piece as finished, Marilyn.

It was a moment of grace.

In that moment, I gave up my need for sadness, my love affair with desperation and fear.

That year was the first time I saw spring come. *Oh is this how it has been all along, with the pink and white buds pushing out the ends of the branches, and the sweet smells in the air? How can I be thirty-three years old and just now noticing?*

In disbelief, I heard friends say, I love you, and amazingly, I loved them, too. I continued writing. And somewhere deeper than consciousness, I made another important decision the last day of Wendell's class: when I walked out of that classroom, I knew that my marriage was over.

❧

I continued my work with Wendell, doing independent study. Once I happened into him in front of the elevator, and while we were both waiting, I said spontaneously, Wendell, you changed my life.

He would have none of it. He said, No, I didn't change your life. You changed your life. I just asked you to use words well.

It is a dangerous endeavor, using words well, as I discovered. All the changes that came were not easy, not for me and not for others. My story is not a fairy tale where everyone lives happily ever after—it is a messy human story.

❧

Frank had been called out for an emergency, a gunshot wound. The usual stuff for a surgeon on Saturday night. The boys were in bed, and I had the luxury of the big house and the fireplace all to myself. The fire was burning low. I stirred the glowing logs with a poker, and watched the flames flare up again. I lit the two candles in the brass candlesticks on either end of the mantelpiece and turned out all the lights. Then I sat cross-legged in front of the fireplace, pulling my old green afghan around my shoulders, and watched the orange and yellow tongues licking at the wood. Consuming it.

I wanted an undefinable *more*, and that wanting grew daily, like a hunger, but a hunger without a name. A familiar voice bearing a load of guilt came at me. *How many women would give anything to have what you have? A good man, a genuinely good man, who is absolutely devoted to you and the boys. A three-story Victorian home, perfectly restored, filled with antique furniture, lined with lace curtains. All the money you care to spend. And in-laws who have taken you in as their own child. How can you be so ungrateful? Are you out of your mind?*

Why could I not love Frank? What did it mean to love a man, anyway? I do love him, I thought. But I don't *love* him. *Frank is like a mooring when I'm venturing out. He doesn't question what he's doing, or why. He knows. He has always known that he wanted to be a doctor in a small community in Kentucky and raise his children—four of them, if I am willing. But what do I want? I have no idea. I never thought to ask.*

The voice kept on, not letting up: *You will lose everything you care about. How do you propose to take care of yourself? Don't think you'll have any defenders—everybody loves Frank. He's such a fine man. And you will hurt the people you love the most: the boys, Frank, Frank's parents, Frank's sister and her husband, your parents, your brother and sister, friends. And all because of your selfishness and immaturity. If you knew what you wanted, what you hope to gain, that might be different. You just know that you don't* feel *married. Is that any reason to get a divorce?*

I saw that the fire was getting low, and I needed to feed it. I added a few smaller branches to tempt the flames up again, and then a couple of larger logs. The breath from the bellows brought the fire back.

Divorces are necessary sometimes, I thought, when the spouse is a hopeless alcoholic, say, or when he beats his wife or kids. Or maybe even if the two can't get along, and they scream at each other day and night. Divorce could even be justified, perhaps, if one partner refused to ever have sex. But none of this is even remotely the case with us. You don't divorce someone you've never even had a fight with.

The previous night I had tried once again to talk with Frank about my bad feelings. I began in the usual way: Frank, I want to talk about . . . about our relationship.

As was his pattern, Frank sighed, looked away, and listened silently while I talked, while I cried. He never said anything, though, except just to reassure me that *he* was happy. He thought we had an exceptionally good marriage. I can't imagine being married to anyone else, Frank had said. *But how can we have a "good marriage," if I am so miserable? How can he be so happy if he is married to me, and I am so unhappy?*

I heard the key in the back door. Poo-o-o-o, came Frank's voice. The sound of his footsteps brought him closer and closer to the living room, into my sanctuary. Hi, Honey. How's my sweetheart? He bent to kiss the top of my head, and as he took off his coat, he added, Looks like your fire is about out, isn't it.

CHAPTER 41

in which I declare my work

No one knew about my writing. Frank knew that I was taking a writing course with Wendell Berry, but he never asked me what I was writing about. Not that I would have told him, or anyone. I kept my writing in neat stacks in the lower kitchen cabinet next to the fridge, along with my old red Webster's dictionary from college. The cabinet was my secret hiding place, like the one I had had as a child, where I tucked away strands of ribbon and pretty stones I found in the street.

When the children were asleep or at preschool, I would sneak into the cabinet, greedy for the touch of the paper, for the sharp pencils, for the words. I would make a cup of good coffee for myself, and sit there in the silence, with just the hum of the refrigerator for company. The scratching of the pencil on the paper was like some kind of primitive music to me, like the shaman's rattle, connecting me with the *whole*. Writing was a descent into unfamiliar waters, where lovely and fearsome creatures of various shapes and colors appeared and disappeared, leaving me changed with the meeting. There was no end to the adventure, or to the longing that drew me there.

I thought my hiding place was safe from Kash and Madison, but even as toddlers they had this way of always knowing my heart, which they wanted for themselves alone. Late one afternoon when I had been upstairs cleaning the bathroom, I came downstairs to find that the boys had pulled all of my manuscripts out onto the kitchen floor. My pencils were scattered over the linoleum. My dictionary was flopped open, and Kash was sitting on one end of it, thin paper full of words bent under his bottom. Both boys were busily coloring the pages of my writing with their crayons. Look, Mommy! Madison said proudly, holding a red-scribbled sheet up to me as I entered the room.

No-o-o-o! I screamed. No-o-o-o! These mine, mine! You can't have them! A deep growl, an animal sound, emerged from somewhere. I had my hand in the air, to strike my boys.

Kash and Madison began screaming, No, Mommy, no! and moved away from my rage. I stopped suddenly, and composed myself. Come here! I ordered. Stop crying, and listen. This is Mommy's *work*. I paused, surprised at this last phrase. This is Mommy's work, and you must never, never touch it again. Do you understand? They continued to whimper. Do you? I said. They nodded their curly heads in unison. Go to your room and stay there until I call you for dinner.

I bent over the ruined papers, collecting and sorting, restoring order. As I did, I began to cry, splashing big tears on the very papers I was trying to save. *Who is this women with her desperate need for paper, for words? Where will this fury, this longing lead?* But the astounding declaration remained: *This is my work. This is my work.*

CHAPTER 42

in which I struggle to stay in my marriage

SINCE THAT LAST CLASS WITH WENDELL, EVERYTHING HAD CHANGED. In short, I didn't feel married anymore. When someone would introduce me as Frank's wife, I felt like an impostor. At the same time, I didn't want to consider divorce. I had created a family, a home, a place in the world, and I didn't want to give all that up. Maybe counseling would help, I thought.

Our first marriage counselor was a clinical social worker—she was skilled, but we stopped after the session in which she invited us to hold hands and look into each other's eyes. I realized that I did not want to hold hands or look into Frank's eyes. I didn't want to be close to Frank.

The second counselor was a psychologist, trained in Gestalt work. We saw him for only one session. He was unnervingly blunt. Near the end of the fifty minutes, he said, Are you happy in your marriage? What could I say but no, and he responded, Well, why then would you want to stay married?

The third was a Christian counselor named Dr. Gladman. He must have been in his early 70's, I guessed. His white hair was perfectly coiffed, his blue eyes unwavering. His tie had ducks on it. Flying ducks. Except for the tie, he could be on TV, I thought. Selling soap. Or religion. I couldn't remember who had recommended him. Some friend had said that he was an emeritus in the Religious Studies Department at the University of Kentucky, and often talked with couples who were "having problems." I wanted a path back into the marriage, if I could find one.

Dr. Gladman offered a warm hand to me and then to Frank and asked us in. His mouth stayed in a kind of perpetual smile. Such flagrant happiness has always been suspicious to me. I looked around. *Everything in order.* He had a sign on his desk that read "God isn't through with me yet," and pictures of his children and grandchildren and his late wife, Eileen. He told Frank and me about losing Eileen two years before, to cancer. For months he did not want to live, he said, still smiling. The thing that pulled him out of this dark place was listening to the Moody Blues. For hours, he would just sit and listen, he said, until one day the sadness was all washed out of him.

Well, what seems to be the problem? he asked, looking at Frank. Frank explained in the simplest of terms that *he* didn't really have a problem, but that I was unhappy and wanted to leave him. His problem was that he didn't want me to leave. Dr. Gladman cocked one white eyebrow, widened his smile, and turned to me. And what might make a pretty young woman like you want to do a thing like that, Marilyn? He was smiling as though he knew something I didn't know.

It was hard for me to say why I wanted to leave the marriage. What I said probably sounded stupid to Dr. Gladman. It even sounded stupid to me as I was saying it—worse than stupid, it sounded self-indulgent.

Well, I'm—I'm not *attracted* to Frank. We don't have fun together.

Fun? His blue eyes were staring me down, and a subtle smile was playing along his mouth.

What I mean is, I said, trying to understand my motives even as I was speaking, what I mean is, I don't like being with Frank.

You don't like talking with him? You don't like making love with him? What exactly do you mean? Dr. Gladman's voice rose. His eyes widened.

No, it's not that. I like talking with him. We talk about things.

Politics. Movies. Our sex life is OK. I stopped to think. I mean, well, it's like the real me isn't there when I'm with Frank.

Dr. Gladman looked at Frank, who just shrugged his shoulders. What do you mean, "the real me"? he asked.

It's hard to explain, I continued. When I'm with Frank, I'm just Frank's wife. Kind of an appendage. Do you understand? Dr. Gladman looked at me with a vacant stare.

Finally he spoke. I'm remembering my own marriage with Eileen. She was my wife, yes, but no appendage of me. We were equally tied together, serving each other and God. We were one. His eyes grew misty. Yes, she cooked my meals, cleaned our house, even packed my bags for trips, and tucked little candies that I loved in the side pockets—she was utterly devoted to me—but I never thought of her as less, in any sense of the word. I certainly never considered her an appendage.

We have a maid, said Frank.

What? said Dr. Gladman, returning to the present.

We have a maid, repeated Frank. Marilyn doesn't have to clean the house. She cooks, but she doesn't have to. I don't care. She can have a career if she wants one. She knows that.

I was squirming in my chair. I'm not talking about cooking or not cooking, cleaning or not cleaning, I said. I'm not talking about career or not career. I'm talking about relationship. Frank is at the center of everything. He's not pushy or a bully. He's a nice man. But he's at the center, and I am at the periphery. I'm the doctor's wife. The name says it all. I'm Mrs. Frank Sewell, Jr. It's printed on my stationery. That's my identity, and it has been ever since I got married. Whoever I am is shut down. I feel dead. I'm depressed all the time. I could feel my ears beginning to burn, my breath coming quickly.

Dr. Gladman stopped smiling. Depressed? he said. I can see why, Marilyn. Can't you? You're about to throw away the dearest thing in your life: a good man who loves you. He looked down and shook his head. He drummed his fingers on the desk for a moment and then turned his blue eyes on me once more. Now think back.

Why did you marry Frank to begin with? Was it not for certain qualities of character that he still possesses? Didn't you love him and honor him and want to be his wife?

No, I said. I mean, yes, I married him for qualities of character, as you say. But I didn't love him the way I want to love a man. I told him that all along, but he wanted to get married anyway. I said to him, It'll have to be I need you rather than I love you, and he said all right. I think he never did really care whether or not I loved him, he just wanted me to marry him, which is something I never understood. But I did it, and I did it because I wanted a home and kids. I was lonely. I wondered if I could ever love any man—I mean I never had except for my Daddy. So if I couldn't love anyone, I might as well marry Frank because he is a good man, and would be a good father I knew, and a good provider, which he is, and he says he loves me, even though I have trouble *feeling* that he does, but then of course I have trouble believing that anyone loves me. I paused. So maybe our trouble is all my fault.

H-m-m-m-m, said Dr. Gladman, knitting his bushy white brows. H-m-m-m. He was pushing his fingertips together, tensing and relaxing, tensing and relaxing. I noticed the nails. Slightly blue. But perfectly clipped. Frank, what do you have to say about all this?

Frank didn't say anything for a while. Then he spoke in his kind, quiet voice: I think Marilyn loves me. I think we have a happy marriage. He paused. You know, sometimes I look at the wives of some of the men I know, and I wouldn't want any one of them. I'm so glad to be married to Marilyn.

I usually felt guilty when Frank talked like that. But that day for some reason I felt angry. I wanted to remain calm, composed, but I felt my heart pounding, and my voice began to rise. How can you say we have a happy marriage when I'm walking around depressed all the time? I'm one half of the marriage, aren't I? Well, aren't I? And how can you be glad to be married to a depressed woman who tells you all the time she doesn't love you? How can you? I sighed, and my shoulders fell. I'm sorry, Honey, I'm sorry, I'm sorry. Frank didn't move. He didn't look at me. He didn't say anything.

I think you do love Frank, said Dr. Gladman softly. What is love, anyway? Is it fireworks and passion all the time, or is it just caring, like you just expressed?

I thought about what he said. I do care about Frank, I said. I love him as a friend. I love him as the father of my children. I struggled to find the words. But—but the deepest part of me, the essence, is not present in this marriage. There is no place for it, for *me*, in the marriage. It's a spiritual something that's missing. And so when I'm introduced as Frank's wife, I know it's a lie. I'm living a kind of lie by being in the marriage, because my truest self is not there.

Frank was still silent. The air seemed thick, heavy. Turning to me, Dr. Gladman offered a summary of his findings: Marilyn, you fantasize that you could find a better man than Frank, but Frank suits you. You are a dependent personality, my dear, and you will always be a dependent personality. You will always yearn for someone to take care of you, and you will never trust anyone who tries. Frank is a good man, and he loves you. If you leave him, you may end up with someone half as good. Or with no one at all. His mouth had become a stern line.

I felt a sharp pain in my heart. I kept hearing his words again and again: *you are a dependent personality, and you always will be.* Yes, I did feel dependent. Yes, it was difficult for me to trust. Yes, I knew Frank loved me. Maybe I was too sick emotionally to be able to love anyone. Maybe I would feel lost and alone whether I was married or single, whether I was with Frank or some other man. Maybe all this stuff about my "true self" was just a rationalization for an inability to get close to anyone. Maybe I could not love Frank because I could not love.

I have to go, I said. Thank you very much, Dr. Gladman. I stood to leave, and Frank stood with me.

Well, I hope this session has been helpful. I'd hate to see you lose all you've got here, both of you, said Dr. Gladman. He turned to Frank and offered his hand. Good luck. If you want to see me again for another session or two, please feel free to call. I enjoy doing this kind of thing. Then he looked at me. Remember that God wants what's best for you, Marilyn. Nothing less.

He smiled and patted me on the back as I turned to go, adding, I'll keep you in my prayers.

CHAPTER 43

in which my body takes the lead, with consequences

Why does he have to leave on New Year's Day?

I didn't want him to go then. I wasn't sure when I wanted him to go, but not then. Holidays were bad enough without a marital separation. It was practical, Frank had said. He needed to start his new practice in Harrodsburg.

The couples Frank and I socialized with at Central Baptist would be having a New Year's Eve party. They did every year. But we had not been invited this time. After all, nobody wants New Year's Eve to be funereal. And besides, the church was not looking favorably on me for leaving Frank.

For our last dinner together, I broiled a trout for Frank. It was his favorite food, after all. As I slid the sleek, dark fellow under the broiler, its wet black eye seemed to stare at me. I imagined it as it once was, gliding peacefully through calm waters, making its easy way around submerged logs, exploring underwater caves. I always felt guilty when I cooked a whole fish. Fillets were easier on my conscience.

Frank ate the meal in silence. Good fish, Marilyn, was all he managed. *How can he be so calm? It would be easier if he were mad.*

After dinner, he gave the boys their bath and then played with them, rolling and tumbling on the blue sea of carpet in the front hall, a nightly ritual for them. As I put the dishes in the dishwasher and wiped down the counter tops, I heard the boys' laughter and squealing. *They don't really understand that he's going, what it all means.* Frank put the boys in bed, and then retreated to the living room with his medical journals. The usual.

You're reading? I said.

Frank looked up. It was perfectly obvious that he was reading. Yes, he said.

Well. Well, yes, I guess you are, I said.

Yes, he said again.

Do you want to talk?

He paused before he spoke. About what?

Oh, anything, I answered. About us, maybe.

No, he said.

Are you sure?

I don't know what to say, Marilyn.

Well, I know this sounds stupid, but I'm going to miss you.

Frank stared at the floor. I love you, Marilyn. I'll probably always love you.

Yes, I said, nodding. I felt myself filling with the kind of love I had always had for Frank, a combination of gratitude, affection, respect. I wanted to say, I love you, too, Frank, but I could not. How then could I explain to him or to myself why I had to leave? Instead, I asked, Do you want to stay up for the New Year?

No, he said.

We had not made love for a couple of months—there was too much hurt and uncertainty between us. That night we fell asleep in each other's arms, as we had always done during our six years of marriage, curled into tight question marks, Frank with his arms wrapped around my body, his hands cradling my breasts, my hands on his hands. I wondered why I was turning away from this man. I wondered if any man would ever hold me like this again. I didn't plan to make love. But we made love.

⚜

In the morning she is still wrapped tightly in his arms, her back turned against him, his face nuzzled in the curve of her neck, under her dark hair. Not wanting to wake him, she slowly takes his arm from round her and slips delicately from his grasp. His arm rests in the empty place where she had lain. She looks at his sleeping face and thinks that she loves him. Maybe there is another child, even now, growing inside me, she thinks. Maybe I'll have to stay.

CHAPTER 44

in which I must choose, and I choose myself

YOU'RE A MATURE WOMAN AND CAN STAND A LITTLE PAIN, SAID THE NURSE matter-of-factly. Her body was round and steady. Not like some of these young kids we get here. We have to put them under. But you've had babies. You know what pain is. It's safer without the anesthesia, you know. Now, strip everything off, and put this on, she said, as she handed me a white paper gown. The tie goes in the back.

I agreed about the anesthesia. I had accepted that the pain would be part of the procedure. I wanted to be conscious when it was happening. I wanted to be fully awake.

I looked around the room. The walls and porcelain fixtures were white; the cabinets and containers were stainless steel. There was no color anywhere. They could have done with a poster or two, I thought. Maybe a travel poster, or something. I stripped down and waited.

The nurse returned with an aide. This will be an easy one, she said. You're just nine weeks along. There should be no problem. It'll be over in a few minutes. The aide wheeled me out the door, down the corridor, and into a larger room that was outfitted with bright lights and the machine that was to be used.

I was no sooner rolled into place than I was struck with a deep urge to get up off the table and run. *They are going to kill it.* My hands gripped the sides of the table. *You're getting a divorce! You can't have this baby!*

I was trying not to cry, but tears kept squeezing out the corners of my eyes. Everyone would feel uncomfortable if I cried, I thought. The doctor came in, and seeing my tears, turned his eyes first to the nurse and then to me. He put his hand on my bare foot and asked softly, Are you all right?

Yes, I said, nodding my head, my face wet and twisted with pain. Yes. I just wish it didn't have to be this way. The doctor nodded, and patted my foot. Move down on the table a bit, he said. Move closer to me.

Don't think about it, Honey, said the nurse, as the doctor made ready. Think about something else. What are you interested in? I had no answer. What are your hobbies? the nurse persisted, and she took my hand. I needed to offer something.

Antiques, I said.

The whirr of the machine began, like a giant insect, and I heard under that sound the voice of the nurse droning on and on about antiques. Ice cupboards, milk glass, grandfather clocks.

At last it was finished. I was wheeled back to the white and gray room, to rest before the trip home. I expected that I might feel empty. Or maybe sad. But I didn't. I didn't feel anything at all.

Not that it was over, or would ever be over, for I had imagined that the child would have been a little girl, a daughter, and each year that went by I knew my loss, and I knew that I would never have another. I wondered what my daughter would have been like— perhaps like me, but happier I thought, full of smiles, and prettier.

Just recently the question came once again. The gyn nurse at the clinic where I go for my routine care never fails to begin my yearly check-up with the question, How many pregnancies? How many births? Each time I have wanted to say, Three. Three pregnancies and three births, I have three children. But instead I am reminded that I refused a life, that I had the power to choose, and I chose for myself, and I will never know whether or not I took the better part.

CHAPTER 45

in which I find a church home

DIVORCE BRINGS A PLETHORA OF SATELLITE PROBLEMS FOR A WOMAN, MOST of which I did not anticipate. I did not anticipate losing my credit. I did not anticipate being propositioned by my best friend's husband. With a BA and two master's degrees, I did not anticipate being unable to get a job that would pay a living wage. And I did not anticipate being rejected by my friends at Central Baptist Church in Lexington or being rejected by the church itself. My learning curve got steeper every day, as social and economic structures shifted and changed with my new status.

I was in my therapist's office one day, weeping as I told her of the collapse of my entire social structure, when she threw out a suggestion. She said, Why don't you go over to the Unitarian Church—there are a lot of divorced people over there.

I didn't know anything about Unitarians, but I thought I would try them out. I needed people in my life, and I needed a church.

For my first visit, I did not attend the Sunday service—I went to the volleyball party the church sponsored every Friday night at the University of Kentucky gymnasium. When I arrived, a game was underway and other players were waiting their turn, sitting in a row on the shiny wooden floor. I sat down cautiously on the end. Time after time, a game would end, and those waiting would rush up to take their places for the next game. Too shy to move, I just sat and watched.

All of a sudden, I felt a figure looming over me. I looked up and saw a black man with an engaging smile. Later I would find that his name was Titus and that he was a graduate student from Africa. He said, Don't you want to play?

Nodding, I whispered, Yes.

Well, come on then, he said, and he reached down to me, offering his hand, pulling me up from the floor and into the game. That's all it took—I was in. Soon I was attending all the Sunday services and participating in the social events. I had found my people.

This incident may not seem extraordinary, but for me, in that time and place, it was. Growing up in the South, I had never before been in a church where black people were welcome. I was taught to fear black men. Titus, a stranger, reached down to me, taking my small white hand into his large black hand, and pulled me into new life. For Titus, his gesture was ordinary and everyday, nothing special. For me, it was definitive, full of the keenest kind of irony and full of hope.

In the Southern Baptist church, I could teach a Sunday school class or sing in the choir, but I could never become a deacon— spiritual leadership was reserved for men. My experience at the Unitarian Universalist church could not have been more different. Both men and women were leaders, both men and women could be parish ministers. Little did I know it, but in the moment that I took Titus' hand, my journey toward ministry had begun.

I consider, as perhaps all of us do, what if. What if my therapist had not mentioned the Unitarian Universalist church? What if I had decided not to go to the volleyball game? What if I had felt that this strange new faith was too frightening to explore? Or what if I had simply left that evening, having been unnoticed by anyone? What if, for whatever reason, Titus had failed to reach out to me?

It was true, as my therapist said, that there were a lot of divorced people in the Unitarian Universalist church—and others were exploring open marriage. It was the '70s, a decade of social experimentation in the culture at large, and Unitarian Universalists, as always, were some of the first to question the status quo and try out new ways of being. Partners were shifting and changing before my very eyes. I was surprised, but in no position to judge, as I was in an exploratory mode myself—and besides, I had had enough of judgment for a while. From the Unitarian Universalist church, I gained acceptance and love and community, all of which had been in short supply in my life. And I was invited to learn, to teach, to lead.

We become ourselves by the most circuitous, unpredictable, accidental, astounding routes. Or do we? Perhaps, as some would say, the way was meant to be.

CHAPTER 46

in which I enter into the wilderness

In 1972, anthropologists George and Nena O'Neill published *Open Marriage*, declaring that married couples should have the freedom to engage in sexual relationships outside of marriage. They did not suggest cheating on your spouse but argued that the healthiest marriage is one in which each partner has room for personal growth and can develop outside relationships. The book sold over 1.5 million copies and was on the best-seller list for forty weeks.

The term "open marriage" came to be synonymous for non-monogamous marriage, which is not at all what the O'Neills intended. Nevertheless, the book marked the beginning of a large-scale questioning of the relationship of marriage to sexuality—not just among young "hippie" revolutionaries, but widely, too, among the middle class. When the sexual dike burst, it seemed that for many educated and respectable people, everyone was available to everyone else sexually. It was that golden age after the sexual revolution of the '60s, but before the onset of AIDS.

Frank and I separated on the cusp of this phenomenon. I didn't go along with the O'Neill's advice, and in fact wrote a review of their book saying so. Nevertheless, like so many others, I began to think about sex and relationship in an entirely new way. Sex was more about fulfillment than covenant, more about joy than duty.

As a single woman, I explored this opportunity to learn about men and about sex—and to figure out the relationship between sex and commitment. My sexual adolescence took place, then, not when

I was a teenager, or even a young adult, but when I was a mother in my mid-thirties. Looking back now, I see a woman who was naïve, even embarrassingly foolish at times, but all the while discovering and learning. During this period, I was full of the joy of living.

ॐ

After Frank moved out, I carved a fifty-by-twenty foot swath out of the rich bluegrass soil in the backyard, and retreated to my garden for six months. I grew all manner of vegetables there—carrots, string beans, beets, okra, tomatoes, green onions, peas, even cauliflower and brussels sprouts. Flowers bloomed in some of the rows and around the edges of the garden, hardy flowers like marigolds and zinnias. I liked to look out over the tidy rows and admire their orderliness and beauty. Somehow having my fingers in the dirt—planting, watering, pulling out weeds so that my tiny plants could live—made the loneliness seem all right, a part of what must be. And so most every day in the early evening, as the sun was losing its power to burn, I knelt down in the black earth.

Then one night at a church party, I met a man. He had a kindly smile, clear blue eyes, and just the wispiest sort of a sandy-colored beard. When I noticed this man, he was busy opening a beer. I looked directly at him and asked, What is your name?

The conversation went from there, and the next day, we played tennis together. I wore my sexiest tennis outfit—peach-colored, with a plunging V-neckline and a flouncy little skirt. I felt his eyes on my body the whole afternoon—which is, of course, precisely what I had invited.

We had dinner together that night, and I began feeling stirred in the same way as when I first started dating, in my college days. And yet this encounter was different: I knew the pleasures of love-making now, and that possibility was pulling at me. What was the protocol, though? I had not dated for years, had never made love with anyone other than Frank.

After dinner, we found ourselves sitting close on the living room sofa and talking. I was agitated, unable to concentrate on the conversation. *When is he going to make his move? Does he want to go to bed with me? What should I do, if he does want to? Is it too soon?* My questions were crowding the space between us. Finally he reached over and put his hand on the back of my neck and gently kissed my lips. I looked away, feeling almost as shy and confused as when I was first kissed in front of my college dorm, twenty-five years before. I hardly knew this man, but I wanted him. *My God, what happens next?*

His left arm was around my shoulders, and his right hand moved to my blouse. He unbuttoned the top button, one of fifteen tiny buttons down the front of the blouse. I pulled back, expecting that he would then pursue. But to my surprise, he stopped. I would like to make love with you, he said, but not if you don't want to.

I was taken aback. *You mean, I have to decide?* I confessed to him that I was feeling scared and confused, that I didn't know what I wanted to do. So he just accepted that and didn't make any further move. *What do you do with a man if he doesn't insist?* To admit that I actually wanted to go to bed with this man seemed distinctly unfeminine—I was a Southern woman, trained to be coy with men. And yet I realized, after a few minutes of pondering, that his approach made me feel free and grown-up in a way I never had before. That felt good. I paused, took a deep breath, and looked at him. I'd like to make love with you, I said.

Are you sure?

Yes, I'm sure.

He handled the other fourteen buttons very nicely, and we went upstairs to the bedroom. I'm a gentle lover, he said. And he was.

I was never to see this first lover again—I had known that shortly after meeting him. On Sunday morning I'm moving to Michigan, he had said. And his going was all right. In fact, it was just right: he would remain in my memory as one who taught me a different way with men and who loved me gently all through the night.

CHAPTER 47

in which I learn to dance

I BEGAN WAKING UP TO FEELINGS THAT I DIDN'T EVEN KNOW WERE THERE. Like the anger I had at Frank. I hadn't even known I was angry. Needing to sort out my feelings, I started attending a Gestalt therapy group every Tuesday afternoon at the University. Should I divorce, or not? I was edgy, impatient. I asked a friend who was a psychology professor where I might go to have a more inten- sive experience, to help me get my head clear. He told me about a Gestalt therapist from Kalamazoo named Neil Lamper. He didn't know Neil personally, but he knew people who knew him. He said Lamper offered a two-week workshop at a farm called Tuwakachi, near the small town of Allegan, Michigan. I asked about Neil's background and reputation, and my friend said that he had a Ph.D. in educational psychology and had trained with Fritz Perls. He added, People say he's a little crazy, but creative. I laid plans to go.

The drive to Michigan was in itself a challenge, since Frank had done virtually all the driving during the years of our marriage. On the Sunday before the workshop was to begin, I set off in the red Volvo, and once I actually started down the road, I began to feel strangely light, and free. I allowed myself to smile and let go of the guilt—*at least until this workshop is over.* I listened to country music on the car radio. I liked country music: it's about real life, about things like betrayal, death, and adultery.

Michigan! Corn country. There were acres and acres and acres of the green waving stuff, and a sky much bigger and bluer than any

I had ever seen. By the time I was ten miles from Allegan, though, rain clouds were gathering. I had a map that Lamper had sent me showing the turn-off to the farm—it was a dirt road, off one of the local blacktopped roads—but I couldn't find it in the pouring rain. After driving back and forth on the main road and then exploring a dirt road to no avail, I finally decided to go into Allegan.

The sky cracked upon, and lightning was streaking down in great white knives, followed by deafening rolls of thunder. The light was strange, unearthly. I could barely see to drive in the deluge—I crept into town at dusk, darkness quickly approaching. Everyone had fled the storm. The streets and sidewalks were bare, and there was no light to be seen in any window or storefront. *Maybe the electricity is off. Maybe even the phone lines are down.*

Cruising slowly to a stop in front of the bank, I decided to wait out the storm in the car. I locked myself in and tried to rest, reassuring myself that I was safe, grounded as I was with rubber tires. At least I wouldn't be struck by lightning. Feeling as if I were in some weird science fiction movie, I dropped off into a fitful sleep.

I woke at daybreak to an incredibly bright sky. My clothes were rumpled and felt damp, although the interior of the car was totally dry. I found the turn, and then the farm, with little trouble. The muddy red road went straight through miles of cornfields, finally arriving at a group of buildings, the first of which looked to be a barn. I turned off the engine, got out, and tried to get my bearings.

The barn was an old gray weather-beaten structure, with the name "Tuwakachi" painted on it in swirling letters of red and blue. An ancient haymaker rested on the ground nearby. No one seemed to be up yet. Everything had an air of unreality to it, as though I had gone to sleep and woken up in a different country.

Seeing a path leading around the barn, I followed it to a more substantial building with a heavy log frame. I pushed open a squeaky screen door and entered the darkness. I paused, took a few tentative steps forward, and then heard a voice say, Hi.

As my eyes adjusted to the dark, I saw a man sitting alone in what appeared to be a dining hall. Slouched in a chair at the far end of a massive wooden table, he was dressed in a faded T-shirt and was cradling a steaming cup of coffee in his hands. I could see that he was a big man, and as I moved closer I saw graying blonde hair and a ruddy face. His mouth turned up on either side as if he were holding back a secret smile, giving him an impish look. His gaze never left my face, but he said nothing else. I stopped about five feet from him, and looked into his eyes. *Who is this big trickster?* You must be . . . I began.

Neil, he said.

🐾

The workshop was intense: three sessions every day, each three or four hours long. The participants, twelve of us, sat on the floor of a huge room furnished only with pillows and cushions of various sizes and hues. Neil did not use pre-planned exercises. He just waited to see who wanted to "work"—that is, to share personal issues or pain with the group.

Neil was about six feet tall with a barrel-shaped chest. He wore the same khaki pants and blue faded tank top every day and rarely had on shoes. He had a restive kind of energy, an animal aliveness, and he got this energy out in little ways, like saying, Yeah, yeah, yeah, yeah, yeah, as he walked about. He liked to tease or jostle in fun. Everyone wanted to please him. When Neil sat down in group, the air was full of potency and possibility.

On the second morning, I had just finished brushing my teeth at the communal sink when I turned and saw Neil standing there looking at me. He said, Hi, and smiled, then walked over and kissed me full on the mouth. I grew wide-eyed, standing as I was with my toothbrush still in hand. *Who was this man who could be so clear and easy, while I doubted my every thought? And who was he to kiss me this way. Wasn't he the therapist, after all?* Neil noted these questions in my face. He just grinned and said, I go after what I want. Then he turned and walked away. Clearly, I was in new territory here, and I had no map.

I found Neil's group work always competent and sometimes downright brilliant. He listened carefully to the words of the person working, but more important he registered nuances of body movement and voice tone. He worked intuitively, using few words, but just the right ones to invite hidden grief or anger or joy. Like with Art, for instance.

Art grew peonies professionally. His specialty was the giant scarlet peony that had won prizes in shows all over the nation. He had pictures, which he passed around to the group the way some people show off their children. But for all the energy that he was able to give to his flowers, he saw himself as a drab weed in the garden of life. Neil picked up on the flower imagery, and by the end of the first week, Art's whole posture and countenance had changed as he began to take on more of the vibrancy of his flowers.

By the third day I felt trusting enough to do my first piece of work. I spoke of the day when I was taken from my mother. I told of knowing her after that only through phone calls that followed her drinking bouts. I told how it felt to live in a home that was not my own, fearful that my brother and sister and I would be put out. That was the ulti-mate threat that Big Papa used when the children misbehaved.

Like the time Donna sharpened her crayons in Big Papa's pencil sharpener. He lined us three children up in a row and demanded to know who had done this terrible thing. Jim and I knew that Donna had done it, but nobody was saying anything. Big Papa started in on us: Well, let me tell you three something. If it wasn't for me and your grandmother you'd be out on your own, and Lord knows what would happen to you poor children, what with your daddy being the no account that he is. Now you listen to me: if you can't behave, we're not going to keep you here. Do you understand? We don't have to keep you here. We're doing it because we love you.

I told about my constant fear for my father's safety. He worked in the top of an oil rig, stabbing pipe, in all kinds of weather, dangerous work that claimed many lives. And often as not, he'd be driving home drunk. Sometimes Daddy would disappear for three or four days at a time, and I would lie awake at night, thinking about him, praying, *Oh, Jesus, please bring him back to us, please don't let him die.* He would stagger in one day, full of white lightnin', and I would bed him down and get his dinner after he finally slept it off. I dared not say anything to him about his drinking--I didn't want to make him unhappier than he already was. *Maybe he will quit if he gets happier. Maybe one day he will quit.*

I finished, and Neil was silent for a long time. Then he looked at me with tears in his eyes and said, I'm sorry it was like that for you. He paused, and then he went on, You are an amazing person. I don't even see how you are here at all. You have yourself together in a lot of important ways.

I took in his words and began to believe them. The other members of the group—Joy and Jim and Florence and Linda and Ernie and Art and the rest—became my allies in believing myself good and strong.

Neil continued to kiss me in his warm, casual fashion, but the kisses became more and more sexual. I found myself standing alone with him one day in the bright sunshine outside the barn, and I said, You know, I'm becoming, well, *uncomfortable* with the way you're kissing me, Neil.

Oh, yeah? he said.

Yes, I mean, I'm becoming *aroused.* Do you understand?

He chuckled. Oh, yeah!

Well, I want you to either follow through, or stop teasing.

I'd like to follow through.

I paused before responding. The problem is that I know you only as the leader of the group, and not as a *man.* I want to sleep with a man, not the leader of the group.

Neil agreed that the "Big Daddy" thing was a problem sometimes, but he said he did not feel that kind of demand coming from me. We left it at that, and parted.

The next day was business as usual, and I kept wondering what Neil was thinking about the previous day's conversation. Each night after our session, the group members put music on, turned the lights way down, and danced, not as couples, but free-form style. On this particular night, someone dared Neil, I bet you won't dance nude. Of course, he wouldn't, I thought. Of course, he did.

Neil wasn't really much of a dancer, but he danced that night devoid of every stitch of clothing, moving his body slowly and awkwardly to the music, thrusting out one arm, then the other, taking a couple of steps, pausing. The room was so dark, I could hardly see his body, just his big form lurching, stopping, plunging, stepping. He didn't enjoy dancing, I realized—but he was encouraging us all to drop the rules and misapprehensions that were keeping us stuck in our lives. As for me, I noted that the world did not fall apart because Neil danced naked. *So what?* That was the night I began to dance alone. I found that there was music in my flesh, all along. *After all, my mother was a dancer, wasn't she?* I let my body—and joy—lead me.

On the following morning, I went looking for a secluded spot to do some reading, and I met Neil on the path. He came shuffling towards me, with his leprechaun grin. I stopped, placed my feet well apart, balanced, folded my arms, and said, Well?

I just jacked off, he said.

I threw my paperback book high into the air and moaned in mock indignation. Neil laughed and moved on down the path for his breakfast.

After evening group was over, Neil suggested that he and I go separately down through the woods to the outbuilding where he was staying. Searching by moonlight, I found the house, tucked as it was in a grove of trees and the tall brown uncut grass of summer. As I entered the rough wooden structure—just one large room, really—I noticed that care had been taken to make the space inviting. The room was dominated by a double bed, over which had been thrown a striped spread of rich earthy colors: browns, reds, deep burnt oranges. There were a rustic-looking desk, two chairs, and a shelf with a few worn books, a clay pot, and a child's doll. On one wall there was a row of nails on which hung a few simple garments. A kerosene lamp gave soft light.

Neil was waiting inside, stretched out on the bed. As I came through the door, he sat up. Come sit with me, he said. I sat beside him, not really knowing what to do next. *Wait and see, I guess.*

Now we may or may not make love, he said. *As if,* I thought. I knew he was trying to make me feel comfortable. He said, Oh, Marilyn, don't you know when I feel about you the way I feel, when you are who you are, there is nothing, absolutely nothing you can do wrong?

Neil seemed to revel in every part of me. He talked to me as he made love, wanting to put into words what he was experiencing, to share the more his pleasure. We finally dropped off to sleep, only to wake a few hours later and make love again . . . then again sleep . . . and again in the morning we made love, as if we would never, could never stop.

I finally got up and walked outdoors, without a stitch of clothing, into the tall wet grass to pee. My body felt relaxed in the same way I imagined it might have been when I was a very small child. I felt a warmth I thought would never completely leave me.

Every night it was the same, and every morning, the same, throughout the rest of workshop.

He told me he loved me. He even said he was in love with me. I wasn't sure I could believe him, though. I knew he had sex with a lot of women. Could I believe him when he praised me, as he did so often? I didn't know.

I did realize that as a therapist, he had no business sleeping with me. It was divisive for the group, for one thing: the leader belongs to all. Many of the participants had been in Neil's groups previously, and they knew they could not persuade him to change his ways, but they resented his behavior and said so. They know we're sleeping together, Neil had told me. So I had to face the disgruntled feelings of the other group members. And oh, yes, I forgot to mention—Neil was married.

The foregoing events could not have occurred so casually a decade later, after the words "sexual misconduct" entered the cultural vocabulary, and after open marriage fell out of fashion. But again, the time was the '70's. What was right, what was wrong? Many of us were dropping the rules in order to find an order that worked for us. And in our searching, we sometimes blundered and hurt others—and ourselves. Mostly, we learned and moved on.

Neil's radical rule breaking was duly noted and roundly criticized by the University of Kalamazoo, where he taught, and in fact the Educational Psychology Department made him take a leave of absence at one point. Nevertheless, his insistence on paying attention to what he wanted and asking others to do the same was healing for many of us. For someone like me, a good girl who was brought up to never speak of her needs, it was a freeing message.

Neil didn't say goodbye. He had told me that he didn't like goodbyes, so I wasn't surprised when he just said, Catch you later, when we parted. As I drove home, my exuberant feelings remained. The Volvo hardly seemed to touch the road. It's not that I was "in love." No, I was changed.

We wrote letters, Neil and I. No abbreviated notes on a computer, because all that hadn't started yet. Neil was . . . well, irrevocably and exuberantly Neil. He was larger than life, and so were his letters. Even now, I don't understand their extravagance. If I shared his words with you, you would doubtless blush or laugh or both. Love letters are meant to be read by the beloved alone.

Neil did workshops all over the country, and from time to time, I set up weekend workshops for him in Lexington. I also returned to Michigan several times to do therapy and to learn Gestalt. But we never made love again. I couldn't get what I wanted from a married man. Besides, I respected marriage too much, and I didn't want to hurt another woman. Neil loved me in his way, which is after all, the only way people can love. And so we were friends over the miles and through the years.

❧

Sometimes you know when someone is going to die, because that person starts wrapping things up, saying goodbye. I should have known that's what Neil was doing when he showed up to see me installed as a minister some fifteen years after my first solitary, searching drive to Allegan, Michigan.

I didn't even know Neil was among the 800 attendees. It was a grand occasion, with me in my red doctoral robe trimmed in black velvet. There were welcomes by the mayor and other noted citizens, prayers, speeches, covenants made, a sermon, music by the choir.

When all the drama was over, the benediction and recessional done, I went to the private room where I was to disrobe, and there he was, waiting for me, with that trickster grin that played upon his face when he was amused. I hadn't seen him in over a decade. He didn't say a word at first, just held me close in his big arms.

When he released me, I saw in a glance the ravages of the cancer and the heart disease he had written me about: his face was lined, his hair whiter, and a front tooth was missing. *Why in God's name didn't he get that tooth fixed?*

After the reception, I insisted that he come home with me and stay for a few days. He had been sleeping at a cheap hotel, hanging out with the down-and-outs on Burnside for three days before the event. Not because he didn't have money. Just because that was his way.

His wife had died and so neither of us was partnered at that point, but sex was out of the question. We were way beyond sex. He had continued to send me love letters full of erotic imagery for years after our sexual relationship was over. He continued, always, to tell me that he loved me.

We talked about . . . well, what can I say? The meaning of life.

Our lives, our choices. What we didn't choose, as well as what we did. All the roads taken and not taken. He told me matter-of-factly about his cancer and his heart condition. He really didn't want to go into the details. He warned me not to let just any man have my heart. He could imagine, he said, that many men would see all that I had to offer—those long legs, yes, even the money I made—and would want me as their own. He told me about his friend Bonnie and her two-year-old and their plans to go to Australia. He had always wanted to live there, he said. And what a great kid—he loved that kid. He didn't spend that much time with his own five kids when they were growing up, and now he just wanted to be with this kid, Bonnie's kid. And Bonnie, well, she was the most sexually uninhibited woman he had ever known.

When he left, he made up his bed carefully, perfectly, without a single wrinkle, and he gave me a gift, Jane Jacobs' *The Death and Life of Great American Cities.* As he turned to leave, he grinned again and said, as I knew he would, Catch you later.

Four or five months later, I guess it was, I got a call from Neil's daughter. I didn't know her at all. She said she had found some letters, and she thought I would want to know. Neil was dead. He had moved to Australia, she said, with a woman named Bonnie and Bonnie's little girl, and two months later, he had a heart attack and died. He always wanted to move to Australia, she said, it was his dream. Yes, I said, yes, it was. And I thanked her for calling me.

That was twenty years ago, twenty years he has been gone. And yet he's still just as much alive in me as he ever was. Way beyond sex, way beyond time. *Catch you later.* So in what sense is he gone? In what sense is anyone ever really gone?

Just a few months ago, I picked up the Jacobs' volume and read it. The time has come round: the man I married is an urban designer, and he's doing a book that takes off where her book ends. Neil would smile, I think.

In my years of ministry, I've been with a lot of dying people. I know how death comes. At the end pleasure will go. The love of good food will go. Dignity won't matter anymore. Even prayers fall away. The last thing a dying person is conscious of is the human voice. Connection is all that is left. We learn that it is all that ever really mattered.

What will we leave behind? Every little thing that we have given. Every little place we have touched in. We have perhaps braided hair. Designed a building. Written a poem. Placed bricks to make a wall. Held a screaming infant. Made a pudding. Saved a stream. Played a violin. Planted a tree. Written a letter. Listened to a friend. Just showed up.

It all remains, way beyond time. *Catch you later*.

CHAPTER 48

in which I open a disco

FRANK AND I SEPARATED WHEN THE BOYS WERE TWO AND THREE. HE moved to Harrodsburg, Kentucky, a nearby town, and started a surgery practice, and the boys and I stayed in our home in Lexington. On weekends they were with their dad. The arrangement seemed to work well.

I loved our Victorian house with its cantilevered staircase and magnificent stained glass windows. But I had always hated the blue carpet flooding the hallway and covering the living room and dining room floors. Wall-to-wall. The same dreary blue wherever you looked. But when a carpet—an expensive, relatively new carpet—claims a space, it's hard to think about just ripping it up. Taking up the tacks, turning the raw underside up for all to view—it would seem like a violence. The carpet was there, fixed. I thought I was the one who needed to adjust.

It took my friend Benjamin to think of a solution. He wanted to see my house, so I invited him over for a beer after our tennis match one day. I opened the huge sliding door to the dining room, evoking an aching sound from the wood. I said, I never use this room anymore. It's a shame. All this wasted space. I surveyed the relics of my life: the Regency table, and my prized Chippendale chairs, the sideboard and the china display case. Benjamin took one look, spun around on his heel, did a funny leap into the air and said, How about a disco?

What do you mean, How about a disco? I asked, incredulous.

Just what I said. Turn it into a disco. You love to dance so much.

He was serious. And what he said about dancing was true. Ever since Tuwakachi, I had loved dancing.

It's easy, Benjamin said. First you sell the furniture. You should get a dandy price for *this*, he said, rapping the dining table with his knuckles. Then you pull up the rug, with a little help from our good folks at the Unitarian church, and throw it in the attic. Then we all have a pizza party and sand the floor and stain it. Done. That's it. When do we begin?

But you don't understand, I said—the furniture is one of a kind. I could never find it again.

But you said you don't use the room at all. So what good is the furniture? This is not a fuckin' museum is it? I mean, your life is *now*, Marilyn. Look at the dust here, for Chrissake, and he ran his finger over the back of one chair.

His logic was impeccable. And yet could I allow myself to tear up the vast blue, to expose the bare wood beneath? Could I let strangers take my lovely chairs? The chairs were rare, works of art. If I sold them, they would be gone for good. There was an order to the room as it now stood, and though I no longer participated in that order, it was there for me, should I want to return. What if I wanted it all back one day?

For weeks the idea nagged at me. But the sliding wooden door stayed closed. Then one evening after I put the boys to bed and I was feeling my loneliness like a sharp, fresh wound, I descended the staircase, pushed open the door, and flipped the light on. It was all still there, in place. I pulled one of the Chippendale chairs back from the table, noting the richness of the red brocade seat. *It's heavy, I had forgotten how heavy.* I sat at my regular place.

Back in my elegant clothes, presiding over my table, charming my guests, I could even hear their words.

This dessert is fabulous, Marilyn! Did you make it yourself? I must have the recipe.

No, I don't take Medicare patients anymore. It's the paper work—it was driving me crazy. Government regulations. And we're going to see more of it—you'll see.

And so then the surgeon said to the nurse, get your tit out of my field of vision, please!

Are you still in the Ladies Auxiliary, Marilyn? Next month we're having a floral designer speak. It's actually a demonstration.

Yes, don't you know—my accountant was dipping into the profits. And a nicer guy you wouldn't want to meet. I'm pressing charges—he'll be cooling his heels in jail if I have anything to do with it.

The Symphony Auction is when—next Saturday, already? Yes, I donated something—a rosewood tea caddy, I think. Early nineteenth century.

The residents work, yes, but not like we did. Remember those days? We thought nothing of thirty-six hours at a run.

The foxhunt is Sunday. Why don't you and Marilyn come to the hunt, Frank? Or at least the brunch after the hunt?

I lowered my head onto my folded arms. I felt as though all my blood had been drained out. I began to have another fantasy—a fantasy of escape.

I am laid out on the Regency table, the way families used to lay out corpses in the old days. I am dressed in white, in a long garment of gauze embroidered with tiny rosebuds, a fresh bouquet of lilies-of-the-valley resting on my bosom, the stems under my long pale hands, perfectly at rest. For once, my make-up is not smeared. My friends file past, handkerchiefs to their eyes, and whisper, Beautiful, What a loss, How sad, and other such expressions. Frank is there, his stony face white with grief. None of them, save Frank, know that I have been eviscerated, my organs donated to the living, that even now my heart is beating in the chest of a retired fireman in the Bronx, promising him a few more years of life, and my liver is making it possible for a Baptist youth minister in Orlando to continue his witness. My eyes have been given, oddly enough, to a Chinese-American student— they peer anew through slanted frames. I have been stuffed with cotton and sewed up rudely with dark thread, my eyelids closed over the same kind of cotton balls I once used to remove my make-up. No one knew just how empty I really was. Beautiful, they say. Just like when she was alive.

Suddenly cold, I sat upright. Hugging my arms around my chest, I fixed my eyes on each piece of furniture in the room, in turn: first the table, then each chair around the table, then the Victorian sideboard, and finally the Edwardian china cabinet, with its delicate floral inlay. *Spindly legs, that cabinet has.* Then my eyes went back to the dining table again. My forefinger moved without any conscious direction to the middle of the table, and I wrote in the dust, in giant letters: D I S C O.

Benjamin was wrong about one thing, though—getting that carpet up and sanding and staining the floor wasn't easy or quick. The whole process took over three months, and though my friends helped, I was the one who ended up on my knees for hours bringing about the necessary transformation. My fingers grew red and raw, the nails encrusted with stain, my back sore. And the job was expensive: I had to rent a sanding machine, and the large floor ate bucket after bucket of the walnut stain. If I had only known when I started . . ., I said more than once.

But the opening night of the disco made me forget all the trials of the conversion. My church friends had made a large blinking sign reading DISCO, which they hung over the doorway. They decorated the room with balloons and crepe paper. One of the men lengthened the wires on the stereo speakers, giving us music for dancing. Everybody brought snacks and drinks to share. We toasted the opening of the disco with champagne, and then we danced until 2:00 a.m. to Little Richard and Chubby Checker and Jerry Lee Lewis and Elvis and all the great music that I had missed dancing to in high school and college. And this was only the beginning of many such nights for me. "Great Balls of Fire!"

꽃

CHAPTER 49

*in which I confront the Southern
Baptists about sex*

AFTER MY FIRST WRITING CLASS WITH WENDELL BERRY, I CONTINUED TO
work with him in independent study. I would get on the elevator
in the Patterson Office tower and rise to the 12th floor to Wendell's tiny office in the English Department, and we would talk.
We always seemed to have plenty of time—although he held regular office hours as required by the university, for some reason
hardly anyone wanted to come see him. Maybe it was because students felt intimidated—his way was to speak plainly, and would-be
writers may have found encounters with him daunting. His office
was painfully bare—no art, no pictures of family, no books, no
nothing. At one point I brought him a little pepper plant to sit
on his desk, the pepper a startling speck of red in the beige and
brown room.

Wendell didn't want to be teaching, I gathered—he likely felt
his farm work and his own writing pulling at him. At any rate, I visited with him weekly while school was in session. We talked about
my writing—and sometimes I told him about my life. He listened,
and often his presence evoked tears. I wrote personal essays, stories
about my upbringing, about my struggle as a single mom, about
marriage—and I wrote about my emerging sex life. He was highly
critical of the latter. The following is a letter I sent, after receiving
a particularly difficult note from him:

Dear Wendell—

Thanks for your letter. I always pay attention to your criticism and advice, whether literary or personal, and I have found wisdom and good sense there most all of the time. Sometimes your words have a peculiar way of sounding obtuse for days or even months and then suddenly they become clear to me. In my present place, however, I find it difficult to understand some of what you said in this last letter . . . .

Your use of the word "fashionable" in regard to my opinions on sex is hopefully not accurate. <However>your last paragraph caused me to think. You speak of good sex requiring responsibility. I'm sure that that statement is true, but the exact application is unclear in my life at this time. What is responsibility for a 35-year-old about-to-be-divorced woman with healthy appetites? Believe me, I'm asking myself. Then you mention that really scary term "self-respect." My life has been about trying to earn self-respect, and so far my method has been restraining myself from pleasure and by working hard and achieving. That plan hasn't worked. And yet I acknowledge that some restraints are called for. I just don't know which ones, in regard to sex. So far I have set up two rules for myself: (1) don't sleep with married men, and (2) don't sleep with a man unless you really want to. I know that's rather loose, but it's a beginning. . . .

The old questions return to haunt me: will I "cheapen" myself? Will I become "promiscuous"? Does he "respect" me? These questions have almost lost their meaning, and so standards are hard to come by.

I want to share with you one other experience I had last week. I went to a Baptist Sunday School leadership conference for single adults. . . . All throughout the conference not one of the speakers had addressed the problem of the Christian single adult and sex. Then finally a female sociologist speaking on "A Lifestyle for Single Adults" mentioned the S-word. Everything became *deathly still. She went on to say that the New Testament clearly teaches that there is to be no sex outside of marriage. (She herself was married, of course.) Then she asked for volunteers to mention alternatives which might compensate for S__, and keep us from temptation. One fellow mentioned "prayer and Bible study." Somebody else said "close friendships," another said "talking," another "sports activities," and one daring person said "touching members of the opposite sex."*

I was just incredulous through all of this, and finally I got up and said, "I'm about to get a divorce. I've been sexually active for eight years, and I plan to continue being sexually active after my divorce. I don't think that has anything to do with whether or not I'm a Christian."

I'm afraid that statement threw an orderly Christian gathering into complete chaos. People were yelling back and forth across the room, mainly at me, but as more entered into the fray, soon it was clear that I was not the only one there who was having S__. The leaders were shaken and unable to control this eruption. The lady sociologist didn't get to finish her "alternatives," and the director of the conference got up and announced that the next speaker had gotten sick. The director then calmed everybody down by saying that it was God's will for us to hear all kinds of opinions and then to be led by the Holy Spirit to our own conviction. After that we had a more orderly discussion of the subject, consisting mainly of personal testimonies from people who had overcome the sin of lusting.

I realized that I would have to fight them on their own ground, so I raised my hand and proceeded to tell them how the Lord had delivered me from the narrow rule-making of my Victorian grandfather. God wants us to have pleasure and to enjoy our bodies, I said. When I realized that God loves me, I was freed up spiritually and sexually. Yes, I have to be responsible, but responsible to the law of love, not to arbitrary rules and ethical standards foisted on us by fearful, guilty people. This impassioned speech was delivered much in the style of the evangelistic preachers I have heard all my life, replete with dramatic pauses, gestures, and shifts in pace and tone of voice. I restrained myself from adding "Praise the Lord!" at the finish of this display.

Maybe I should have told them that when you drop the rules, that puts an awful burden on you. Because it does.

I write this letter not in expectation of a reply, because I am keenly aware of your pressing commitments—I just wanted to share these stories as a kind of response to your letter and your comments on my last essay. Your opinion counts a lot with me— thanks for being my friend.

Affectionately,
Marilyn

CHAPTER 50

in which my mother is found . . . and lost

IT IS A SUNDAY AFTERNOON AND ONCE AGAIN I'M DRIVING THE EIGHTY miles from Lexington to Cincinnati for a visit with Mother. As I enter the hospital parking lot, I note incredulously that the barrier across the entrance will not rise no matter how close I drive the car. The parking lot must be filled, I think, with some relief. I don't have to go in yet. I turn up the volume on the radio and sit there waiting for a car to come out of the lot and make room. I don't hear the buzzing of the ticket machine at all until the motorist behind me knocks on my window and points an impatient finger. I take the ticket out, the barrier rises, and I drive in.

Mother is all dolled up in a sexy magenta gown and peignoir set. I think to myself, She's been waiting for hours. The nurse says, You'll have to come up from Lexington more often—I haven't seen her so fixed up since she's been in here.

I suddenly imagine myself escaping, running out the massive door to Mother's room, racing down the carefully polished hall, and pushing out the double set of big brass doors at the entrance to the hospital—getting out to the air again, where I can breathe. I manage a big smile. Hi, Mother! How're you doing?

Mother's deep brown eyes—the eyes my own so closely resemble—moisten as she reaches for me. I'm OK, Honey, she says. Do you want to see where they cut me? I don't, but before I can answer, she raises her gown and shows a foot-long incision running down her hip, the black thread puckering up the bruised flesh. It reminds me of the way I sewed up the kids' Raggedy Ann—hurried and careless. Purple lines forming corners have been drawn all over her trunk. They make her look vaguely like one of those charts of a cow, showing the various cuts of meat. Those, she says, were for the cobalt treatments, to show the therapists where the machine should go. She has lost one breast, has had a spleenectomy, and now the second of two hip operations, plus all the cobalt.

We talk and talk, about nothing. I ask her what she had for lunch, I ask about Uncle Buddy and his family, I tell her it's cold outside, I ask her, is there is anything, anything at all that she wants. No, there is nothing.

She asks about Daddy again. *She still loves him. She would like to believe that he still loves her and cares that she's going through this agony.* I don't know what to say, how to satisfy her longing.

I am reduced to muttering now. I have finally lasted out the time I have assigned myself, and I tell my mother that I have to go. But Mother is not ready yet. She leans forward and touches my hand and says with great directness, Look, tell me what's wrong. Before you go, tell me what's wrong.

Tears rush in. I'm not even sure what's wrong, so I say what first comes to mind: I'm lonely. I want to be close to somebody. I want somebody to know me and to value what he knows, to value what I am.

Loneliness—yes, I know about that, Mother says. I know all about that kind of loneliness. My problem was that every time I looked at a man, I saw your daddy. She lets herself hurt and then she wipes her eyes with the back of her hand and tries to give me help. I know just what your problem is, she offers. You have a conflict—right? You are too religious a girl, too fine a girl, just to let a man use your body. You want the whole thing—somebody who really cares about you.

I can't right there practically on my mother's deathbed spill the beans about the sexual adolescence I have experienced since my divorce. *I guess I have used a few bodies myself.* Yes, that's basically it, I say. I want somebody who knows me, and somebody who cares.

My mother thinks I'm stuffy, that I just care about books and school. I want her to know that I'm learning to play and celebrate.

I remember the framed picture of Mother sitting on the mantelpiece at home—she is in a chorus line, is all smiles and legs. I've been going to a lot of parties lately, seeing different men. It's been fun, but I'm tired of keeping my brain under wrap and cover. Being the sexy party girl is wearing thin—I have a mind and I want to trot it out and use it sometimes.

Knowing what I know of my mother—how she has always discouraged my academic pursuits as useless at best and potentially harmful at worst—I could have anticipated her response: Play down your mind, Marilyn. No man wants a woman who is smarter that he is. No matter what the libbers say, a man has to feel he is the greatest.

I can't finesse that remark, hurting as I am just now for acceptance I realize not from a man, but from my mother. *Oh, Mother, won't you please look at me before your eyes close for good!*

⁂

I held my mother in my arms before I left the hospital that day, wishing I could say what was in me to say, *the way you dance, the way you love: I am flesh of your flesh, bone of your bone,* but I knew that Mother could not have heard it. Nevertheless, I felt connected to her in a primitive, a profound way that went beyond words. I love you, Mother, I said, and I kissed her rouged face. Mother smoothed back her dark hair and smiled as I turned towards the door. I paused and glanced backwards, some invisible but very palpable bond holding me there. I saw her still smiling. I put my fingers to my lips in a silent kiss, and moved on out the door.

It was to be our last visit, as events fell. Mother died the next week, with no warning—a blood clot, the doctor said, and relatively painless. Her favorite nephew, Dave, found her and she died in his arms. She died in the middle of a raging snowstorm, the worst to hit the Midwest in years, according to the papers. *Wouldn't you know. I couldn't get to her. I couldn't even travel the roads.*

CHAPTER 51

in which Daddy's lack of courage leads to regret

I HEARD THE SOUND OF HIS OLDSMOBILE PULLING INTO THE NARROW drive alongside of the house, and I knew it was Daddy. I was expecting him along about this time, and yet I was surprised that he really did make it, surprised as I always was when he actually came through. I wasn't sure why he wanted to come for Thanksgiving—he had never before invited himself to my house for a holiday, as he always wanted to be free to drink. I was guessing he needed something.

Hey, Sis, he called as he started up the back steps, and I went out to give him a hug.

He's aging fast, I thought. More gray, more lines in his face. But that was not the main difference—it was more the way he carried himself, with a slight stoop, his head lower and his shoulders more rounded. He had always had such a beautiful man's body, and I hated to see him changing this way. He was smaller than he had been.

Hey, Daddy, come on in—do you want some coffee, I just made some for you. I opened the back door and showed him the way through. The strong smell of the freshly brewed coffee filled the kitchen. He sat down at the breakfast table. Are you tired? How was the drive?

He glanced around. The space was bright with its tall ceilings and pale yellow walls and yellow and green scrim curtains at the long windows, where the light was sifting through. The maple tree in its full glory was partly visible through the window. I'm all right, he said. You have a nice place here, Sis, real nice. Where are the boys?

At their Montessori school, they go every day now.

Do you have an ashtray?

Sure.

I got one for him, and then I waited to see what it was he had come one thousand miles to say. I could tell it was confession time, I could see it in his eyes, in the curve of his hands. He lit up a Camel. No more Picayunes, they were long gone by then, I guess, but Daddy would have kept on with them, if they'd still been available, all the better to kill himself with.

He had drunk one cup of coffee and was halfway through the next before he got down to it. His tone shifted, and he left off the small talk, as he stared at the ash burning its way longer and longer at the end of his cigarette. I waited. I had my own coffee to drink.

Well, it sure is strange having your mother gone, he said.

Yes, I said. It sure is.

So that was it. I didn't know how he felt about her death—he had never said anything to me or to Jim or Donna, which wasn't much of a surprise, because he never talked about her when she was alive, except when he was drunk, and then it was always the same. *You know I never loved any woman except your mother,* he would say, and cry, but never when he was in his right mind, just when he was drunk. But maybe then he really was in his truth, it was hard to tell, he gave away money when he was drinking, too, so what was real and what was not real, I never could figure out.

I loved her, you know, Sis, he said, and that's when his tears started. Daddy's crying always made me want to cry, but this time my heart felt stone cold. I remembered how I tried to get him to call her and say something, just anything, when we knew she was dying. She kept asking about him. How is your father? she would say at the end of every phone call or visit, and I would say "just fine," or "the same as always," and she would get quiet then and wait, maybe thinking that if she waited long enough, I might say something she could hang onto, something that might help her get through what she had to go through. But I couldn't give her a thing—he had to do that, and he wouldn't, or couldn't, I don't know which.

I tried to help her, I told her *he always asks about you*, which was a boldfaced lie. I asked him outright more than once to call her and just ask her how she is—that's all she wants, I told him, she needs a little caring, she's not going to be here much longer. But he would always find some reason to change the subject, or leave the phone. She still loves you, I said the last time we talked before her death, she would like to hear your voice one more time, I know it. He said he would call her, but he never did. Instead he came to me, after the fact, wanting me to tell him it's all right, that he's not to be blamed. I knew what was coming.

I wish I had called her before she died, he said. Just then I had this impulse to haul off and slap him right across the face, saw it in my head, just like I had done it, the way his eyes would look and the red prints my fingers would make on his face. I was up to my craw in feeling sorry for him, for all the ways he messed up himself and other people, too, and then came begging for forgiveness, but not the kind of forgiveness where you change your ways and become new—no, he was after the kind where you get shed of your guilt and you go and do the same old shit again. I was sick of it.

I just let him stew in his own juices this time. He was turning his coffee cup round and round, waiting for his absolution, the way he always did—I don't know why he always picked me to confess to. I finally said, You should have. You should have called her.

He shifted the empty cup back and forth between his calloused hands and nodded his head. I meant to, Sis, really I did.

I was quiet, waiting to see what else he could come up with. He bent over and put his face into his arms, and began sobbing out loud. I didn't say a word. My contempt for him rolled up over the edges of me like scalded milk boiling over. I got up and left the room. Went out past that maple, went on to the garden, to breathe. *Let him tell it to somebody who gives a damn.*

I did everything right for the Thanksgiving dinner, I knew how

Granny used to fix it all: the turkey and dressing, the sweet potato casserole with the marshmallows on top, the lime jello salad with fruit cocktail and whipped cream, the hot rolls and pumpkin pie. Everything was the way it used to be at home. I got out the good china and silver, too, just like Granny used to do.

But the main thing on Thanksgiving is that you're supposed to be thankful, which I wasn't. I couldn't muster it up, I was so mad. So I just pretended and went along with what was expected. We had a big dinner like we were supposed to, and the boys played kickball with their granddaddy out in our big back yard, and laughed and shouted under the maple tree. I cleared up the dishes and thought about Mother.

I thought about the day she cut her hand. I was seven and scared, and the red stream ran onto the kitchen floor, and she said, don't ever leave a sharp knife in the dishwater, you'll forget and reach in and cut yourself. Always leave a sharp knife out where you can see it, she said. I try to remember that. There are lots of ways to get hurt—no sense hurting yourself.

❧

I choked on the bitterness inside me that Thanksgiving. She loved my father 'til her dying day. At least he could have told her goodbye.

CHAPTER 52

in which my father kills his wife

I WAS ALMOST ASLEEP WHEN THE PHONE RANG. I WAS TIRED, SO TIRED that I couldn't read anymore, not that night, and just as I put my book down to turn off the light, that was when the phone rang. What I heard was the last thing I expected. It was my brother Jim. I have some bad news for you, he said. Daddy just shot Ruby. Killed her. He's in custody in the Bienville Parish jail. Jim sounded so rational, but then he always did. His voice was tight and quiet, though, more so than usual.

She's dead? I felt a weight crushing back my breath.

Yes, he shot her twice in the chest. Then he called the police and turned himself in.

Why . . . how . . . ?

He came in from fishing real tired, he said. He went to lay down on the bed, on Ruby's white chenille spread, and she said no, to get up off the bed, and he said to leave him alone. Well, she wouldn't and kept fussing at him to get up, and he still wouldn't. She kept after him, and finally he reached underneath the bed where he keeps his rifle—the one he got from Papa, that used to hang in the back bedroom—and aimed it at her and said now I guess you'll shut up and leave me alone, but she didn't believe he would pull the trigger so she just kept it up, saying get your feet off my bed, just like he didn't own anything in the house, he said— well I guess legally he doesn't—and he shot her. Twice in the chest. He was drinking, I guess.

How is Daddy?

Uncle Gene says he's crying all the time, and saying, O Lord, I didn't mean to do it, O Lord, O Lord, over and over again.

Does Donna know yet?

No. I thought you might want to call her yourself.

Yes I will. I'll call her.

I'm going on down to Louisiana to see Daddy and see what I can do to help. Uncle Gene knows everybody in the parish, you know, so Daddy's getting the best treatment possible.

I called Donna, and when Donna heard the news, she couldn't stop crying on the phone, *oh no, oh no*, she kept saying, snatching breath in between wails of pain. I wished that I could cry, but I couldn't. When I got off the phone, I began pacing and growling like some animal that had been wounded and wants to kill. I wanted to slap Daddy's face, and tell him to stop his whining. I wanted to ask why, to tell him that she had loved him the best she knew how, and how could he have done this to her and to the rest the family who had stood by him all these years and loved him.

All my life I had been waiting for just such a message, some message of horror and death, but I was never sure what form it would take. I had thought that maybe my father would kill himself in an automobile accident, or maybe he would be killed in a drunken brawl somewhere in a seedy roadside bar. I thought he might kill another man in a knife fight or kill a whole family by smashing into their car when he was drunk. But I had never guessed that he would go so far as to turn a gun on a woman and shoot her dead.

He finally did it. He finally committed the unthinkable act, the unknown deed that I feared would come someday. But it was worse than I had ever imagined. This murder violated something so deep in me that I felt I could never forgive him. *Never, never.* I was afraid for myself, that there would be a hardness in me that would never go away, that I would never again let love come close enough to betray so much.

I tried to sleep, but I felt as though a great stone had been laid upon my chest, crushing the breath from me. I kept gulping in air, then not breathing, then gulping again. I remembered that Daddy's birthday was just a few days before, and that I had not sent a card. I wondered if I had sent the card or maybe a gift he wouldn't have done this, maybe he felt depressed or alone, maybe I could have prevented the whole thing. That was an absurd thought, I knew, but it wouldn't let me go. I thought about the day of the birthday and how he would feel about getting no card from his oldest daughter, his favorite, I always sent him something, it's just that Frank and I divorced that year, and Daddy's birthday is also Frank's birthday, and I guess I didn't want to remember their day, but I should have, maybe it would have made the difference, I thought.

Finally I fell asleep for a few hours, and when I woke I cried out, a moan it was, full of shame: it was as though I had pulled the trigger. In the South, people always say that bad blood runs in families and I felt tainted as though the blood, her blood were on my hands. I imagined her lying there bleeding from the two great holes where the bullets would have gone out the back and she would be lying in the red stain on her own carpet in that little frame house with the tacky doilies on the end tables and chair backs and her eyes would be open in horror and wonder that her husband, my father, had been willing to shoot bullets into her flesh.

I didn't want to see anyone, to talk to anyone at all, because of the shame I felt all through me—I should suffer, too, should somehow make up for the terrible sins of my father and his father and his father's father. A long, long line of violence had led us here. Had I not heard the story of Uncle Bill, Big Papa's brother, how at the age of only fourteen, he killed a man in Texas?

Big Papa was full of badness, too, all his children told of the meanness that he had visited upon them, and his father upon him, the story goes, and now here I was at the end of that line, thinking maybe I'm bad, too, a bad seed, how could I not be?

I did not want to talk, just to retreat from the world, but there were people to be told. I called Frank. He listened without comment and then mumbled, That's too bad, I'm sorry, and paused and said I'm sorry again and then had nothing more to say. Somehow all those nights in bed together and the two children I birthed, somehow it should have added up to more—I wanted him to be with me in this, even though some paper in some courthouse somewhere said we were no longer husband and wife, what are such words anyway in the face of this sort of thing?

I was too full of shame to tell my friends, even those who were closest to me. How do you tell someone that your father is a murderer, that he killed his wife? It's too much for people to hear. My psychiatrist was the only one I could tell. I told the story over and over, as the weekly sessions went by, sometimes asking him to hold me, which the young doctor did, a resident physician he was, held me like a mother, and finally after several months, the crushing pain in my chest began to ease. The shame and the guilt stayed, though.

I did at last bring myself to tell my closest friend, a tall quiet-spoken woman who moved like a part of the earth, and she, too, held me while I cried out my pain, and that telling made the pain less than it had been, and the guilt.

As for my father, he was kept in jail for several weeks and then released into the custody of his brother, who had been the county farm agent for the past thirty years. Charges were never brought against him, because after all this was a family dispute, it could just as easily have been her that killed him, people said, they did fight a lot, and Ruby was a hard woman, she had quite a temper, they said. Daddy, on the other hand, was everybody's friend, easy to talk to, a really good person, everyone said, so there's no need in him being punished for something that was really more or less an accident—he was sorry for it so why not just leave it at that.

About a week later, I got the following letter from my father, and he included a letter written to him by a young friend:

Dear Marilyn—
I felt like I wanted to tell you how sorry I am all this happened.

I wouldn't have had it happen for the world, honey, I was drunk and out of my head. The truth is that Ruby pushed me to it, though, I was so tired and needed to rest and she wouldn't let me rest, I tried to warn her but she wouldn't pay me any mind. Still I know it was wrong, and I am sorry that you kids have to suffer so much. The little girl who lived next door to us sent me this letter while I was in jail, I wanted you to see it. She has forgiven me, I hope you will find it in your heart to forgive me someday. I love you.

Dear Jim,

I won't you too know that I love you no mater what anyone says you did. I knew It must be by acident, cause you are such a nice mane. I pray for you everday, that you will soon be free. I know you are good in your hart.

Love,

Josie

Right after it happened, Jim and Donna and I went to Arcadia, where Daddy was being held. The jailer was a big man, balding, in regulation tan clothes and shiny black shoes. A huge ring of keys was hanging from his belt, and they jangled whenever he moved. When we asked to see Daddy, he said, Oh, yes, Mr. Fulmer, and kept shifting his eyes away, like he knew that we had never been in a jail before, and were feeling embarrassed to see our father this way. Come on, follow me.

Daddy was in a cell all to himself, which was one good thing I guess, because he was in no shape to have anybody around him. He was sitting on his cot, staring down at the floor, his hands clenched in front of him. When he looked up, I saw that his face was unshaven, his eyes wild and questioning. He didn't have any kind of prison outfit on, though, just his regular clothes. When he saw us three kids, he started sobbing, and couldn't say anything at all. The jailer opened Daddy's cell and let us go in. He cleared his throat. It don't matter to me how long you stay, he said. You all just call out when you're ready to go. He still wouldn't look at us.

Then we were alone with Daddy. Jim and Donna started crying, too, and went and put their arms around Daddy. I watched them, but I didn't move. Part of me wanted to touch Daddy, because he was my daddy and I loved him, but I couldn't feel the love at all, for the sickness in my body. I kept seeing pictures in my head of Ruby lying dead on the floor in a pool of blood and him swaying drunk over her with that gun, and I just couldn't touch him. I didn't say anything.

Jim and Donna went on hugging him and talking to him, *how are you doing, Daddy, are they treating you all right here, do you know when you can get out, have you talked to a lawyer, what does Uncle Gene say,* and so on and so forth. Finally Daddy reached for me, as I knew he would. His good girl.

I'm sorry, Sis, I'm sorry, I'm so sorry that you kids have to go through this.

I've heard it all before. Do you think you can sleep this one off, like one of your usual drunks and shower and dress and go about your business? I pulled back from his touch, and looked away.

Sis, you don't understand. I didn't mean to do it, I swear, she was yelling at me, screaming at me, and she wouldn't stop, and I just went crazy. I didn't mean to kill her. I didn't answer.

Dropping his head into his hands, he started his sobbing again. Jim and Donna were both looking at me, as if to say, *give him something, anything.* But I didn't have anything to give. He whimpered and quieted and told the story.

I had been fishing, been in the sun all day, I was so tired I could hardly see my feet in from of me when I came in, so I just fell into the bed, in my fishing clothes. Ruby didn't want me on her good white spread. She said, Get off Jimmy right now! And I couldn't move at all, but she kept it up, come in there and was pulling on me, saying Get off my bed—I said, get off, and she wouldn't stop, I got so mad I reached for the gun, just to scare her. Now I guess you'll leave me alone, I said, but she wouldn't stop, just kept right on, and I pulled the trigger before I knew it . . . She asked for it, in a way, if she had left me alone, this never would have happened.

She asked for it. Women always ask for it, don't we. He looked at me again, for some kind of response.

It's time for us to go, I said. I called for the jailer, and soon we heard the keys come jangling down the hall.

We went to see Daddy a couple of more times before the funeral, and he kept trying to get me to say he really wasn't at fault, that it was an accident. I wish he could have had enough *character*, I guess you might say, to take the blame. He was responsible for getting drunk, for reaching for the gun, for aiming it at Ruby's heart, and for pulling the trigger. The killing was no accident, like when somebody doesn't know the gun is loaded and that kind of thing. No, it was murder.

❦

Not too many people showed up at the funeral. It was in Ringgold, where they had been living. Ruby had five sons, and they were all there, and their wives and children. A few neighbors and friends. And then our family. Uncle Gene was there, and Aunt Louise, and Donna and I. Jim said he couldn't hardly stand to go.

I don't think Ruby ever went to church, so I don't know where they got the preacher. Maybe the funeral home supplied him. Anyway, the service was short. He talked mostly about Ruby as a good mother, how as a widow she had raised these five sons, sacrificing herself and all. He didn't say anything about her bad temper, of course. He referred to the shooting as a "tragic accident." Nobody wanted to think about it as a murder, even her boys, who had loved Daddy ever since he started seeing Ruby twelve years ago. He taught the youngest one to pass a football, and kick.

Just about everybody who knew Daddy loved him—he was hard not to love.

The graveside was the worst part. The Louisiana sun blinding us, beating down on us in our black and navy blue, the thick moist air so sweet with the cloying smell of mums that I almost gagged. Her sons carrying the casket. The youngest had on those dark-ray sunglasses, but I could see the tears rolling down his face from under the glasses. After they put their mother down, they all lined up on one side of the grave, and our family was on the other. They never said a word to us that day, neither for good nor for ill. That was all right by me. I didn't know what to say to them, either.

※

The boys were in bed, and at last I could take time to make myself a cup of coffee. *Instant. Well, that's easiest.* Since the murder, I had not had much energy. The pressure in my chest continued, and my arms seemed to lose strength. I could hardly open a tight window, or unscrew a jar top.

Taking the whistling kettle off the stove, I looked down at the electric coils, glowing red. I suddenly imagined what it would be like to place my hand on the coils. *White pain, the stench of burning flesh.* The circles then would become scars on my palm and remain there always. *Circles of light. Circles of heat. Circles of desire.*

I looked more closely at the coils. I put my hand over them, feeling the warmth. I took my hand away and looked at the red circles again. *The fires of hell, where souls burn eternally.*

I put my hand out once more, this time closer to the coils. When the heat became uncomfortable, I drew my hand back, turned it over, and looked at my palm. It was dark, scarlet. *Somebody has to pay. I could do it.*

But I didn't do it. I turned away from the stove, and sat down at the kitchen table. I was dizzy, and confused. It was as though I had been shaken from a dream. I might have burned myself, I thought. I might have gotten a bad burn.

I looked at my hands closely. They were lovely hands, really, with long, smooth fingers. These were the hands that dressed the children, cooked their food, touched their faces as I put them to bed at night. My right hand was the one that held my pencil. *I might have ruined my hand. My right hand. My way of loving. God forgive me!* And I put my face down upon my crossed arms, and wept.

CHAPTER 53

in which I say goodbye to Daddy

DADDY WAS NEVER THE SAME AFTER HE SHOT RUBY—HE DRANK MORE whiskey than ever and his flesh, those big muscles from years of working as a roughneck, just melted off his bones, and he began to look positively skinny. His hair was almost all gray, and his hand shook ever so slightly as he held onto his cup of coffee. He couldn't stay still, wanted to move around, like no place was comfortable for him.

He needed somebody and he found this woman—Omega was her name. Daddy always could find women. They came to him, even in his old age. It was something about the way he smiled at some silliness and at the same time opened his green eyes with just enough pain to make a woman want to ease his suffering. It was the way he stood as he smoked, putting his weight on his left foot, leaning forward ever so slightly and cradling the cigarette in his right hand, as if to shelter it from the wind, inviting protection for himself, as he protected the lighted cigarette.

Omega was a widow about his age who lived in the same trailer park where he lived. She wore a gold crucifix every day of her life. Omega agreed to marry him, *wanted* to marry him, the fifth woman in this world to make that choice in spite of the fact that he had driven the first three away with drink and killed the fourth. Omega didn't last long, though to give her credit she did her best—it's just that her heart couldn't stand the stress. Soon after they married, Daddy was pacing back and forth in the trailer and he couldn't even sit still to watch a football game, which was the thing he loved best. Omega didn't know what to do with him, so she took him to the doctor who gave him medication for his nerves, but that just doped him up so much he slept all the time, and so after a while he wouldn't take the medicine. The nights were the worst, because he couldn't sleep, and he would keep her awake all night long. Or when he did fall asleep, he sometimes had dreams that caused him to scream and moan in the dark.

Other times Daddy would go looking through the chest of drawers and throw everything out on the floor for no good reason at all, in a fury, as if he were a boy again, looking for a penknife or a rabbit's foot he had hidden under his socks. If he didn't like the food Omega made—well, in truth she wasn't a good cook— he might turn the plate upside down on the table and light up a Camel and walk on off down the road. Then he would come back home hours later just like nothing ever happened. Omega was the sweet Southern kind of woman who doesn't question her man, just does her best to make him happy, but try as she would Daddy just kept getting worse, and she got worse, too, and finally her children said she had to go in the nursing home or they were going to lose her, and so Daddy was left alone once again.

A few days after Omega left, Uncle Gene called Jim and said that it wasn't going to work for Daddy to live in the trailer any-more because he couldn't take care of himself, and Uncle Gene said he and Aunt Louise couldn't watch over him, and so Daddy would have to go to the State Hospital.

So Jim took a few days off work from his Social Security job and flew on down to Louisiana to get Daddy into the hospital at Jackson. Jim was always the one who could handle him best. My brother was a big man, 6' 7", so he could keep Daddy from getting out of hand, and yet Jim was gentle with him, gentle as a woman. Jim called me after he got back home to Chicago and told me that the hospital looked pretty good, not as bad as he thought it would be—it seemed to be clean inside, and Daddy would be all right he thought, he already was beginning to be the favorite patient of one of the nurses there. That's Daddy for you, he said, everywhere he goes, it's the same.

I didn't want to go see Daddy, but I felt like I should go, because even if he did kill someone, he was still my father and I owed it to him, to at least make a visit. But to tell the truth I kept finding one excuse after the other for not going, until finally Donna called and said let's meet in Baton Rouge why don't we, and drive up together. I knew it would be as hard for her as it would for me, but it would be easier together than alone, so that's what we did.

As we got closer and closer to Jackson, I noticed how pretty and green Louisiana is. I began to feel comfortable the way you are when you grow up in a place—it was so familiar, especially when we got off the big road, more into the country, the way the air smelled, of pine and red clay, and the way the sunlight filtered through the tops of the trees. Donna's old car was in no hurry. We wanted to be in the warmth of that sun as long as we could.

We had to sign in at the guard station before we could go on to the parking lot. They asked us who we were there to see, and we said James Fulmer, and they said who were we, and we said his children. I felt a twinge again with saying that—it's not that I didn't love him or want to see him, it was just the shame again with knowing what he did, and that I came from him. They told us to go right on in to the Geriatrics Ward, and I asked, Geriatrics? because I certainly didn't think of Daddy as being old. His hair was gray, and he was in his late sixties, I guess, but that isn't *old*, isn't *geriatric*, is it? We looked ahead and saw a simple, one-story beige building, not as scary-looking as I had imagined.

Donna and I walked in the double doors at the front, hardly knowing what to expect, and right off some of the patients started trying to bum cigarettes off us. It was pitiful the way they grasped at us, hands shaking, and I was sorry we hadn't brought cigarettes for them. The thing that bothered me most was the way they fixed their eyes on us, not looking away like most people do when they see a stranger. I wanted to do something for them, and there was really nothing to do. I felt a hand grab my elbow, and I turned to see an old black man grinning at me, half his teeth missing, and spittle drooling from the corner of his mouth, mah, mah, mah, was all he could say, and an attendant came and gently pulled him back, saying, Roman, you know better than that, these are visitors come to see James, come on now, come with me, let's go watch some TV, wouldn't you like that, huh? *Wheel of Fortune* is on, you know you like to watch that, and she guided him away.

To get to Daddy's room, we had to pass through the TV lounge. Rows and rows of wheel chairs were lined up there, and other patients in regular chairs, and the huge TV set was blaring away with the music and talk of the game show, but hardly anyone seemed to be watching. Some were looking out the window, others looking at their own hands in their laps, and several had their heads flopped over to the side, asleep. A woman on the end of the last row was putting on make-up. White powder was already caked unevenly on her face, and now she was trying the crimson lipstick, only not just on her lips—she was smearing it on her cheeks and then started to trace it over her eyebrows, too, before one of the nurses saw her and took it away.

Donna and I kept moving, heading towards the nurses' station, and we had to step around a big pool of urine that had not been cleaned up, Donna around one side, and me around the other. My nose was filling with the smell of the urine and Pine-Sol and I began to feel sick at my stomach and wished I didn't have to come here. Why couldn't Daddy have just gone out quick the way some parents do. I could imagine myself coming here for years to see him, trying to comfort him when he is in a place beyond comfort, his brain rotted out with alcohol and his nerves shot with bad conscience. That's all I could see ahead.

The nurses were expecting us, they had Daddy clean-shaven and all dressed up, his trousers pressed, with a clean shirt and red suspenders. I had never known him to wear suspenders—he wouldn't have chosen red, in any case—but I guess they have to worry about patients killing themselves, because none of the patients had belts.

When Daddy saw us, he didn't know who we were right at first, but then we asked him, do you know who we are, Daddy, and his green eyes grew red and filled up with tears, and he nodded and nodded but didn't say anything. So I asked him again, who am I, do you know? He nodded, but I said, I want you to say it, I want you to say my name, Daddy, who am I?

And he said Sis, because that's the name he always called me at home.

I said, that's right, I'm your daughter Marilyn, do you remember, Marilyn Jane—remember I'm named Jane after you, you're James, and I'm Jane, Marilyn Jane, do you remember?

Yes, he said, yes.

Donna was crying by this time—she took his hand and held it in hers and put her face on his hand and kissed it and said, hi, Daddy, this is Donna, you know me, don't you.

He said, Donna.

She said, I love you, Daddy, no matter what, I'll always love you, and he seemed to understand. He nodded and nodded.

Cigarette, he said, and held out his hand.

He was restless and needed to move. The nurse said we could take him for a walk on the grounds, so we did, each of us holding one arm. We walked over to the patients' garden and I asked him if he could grow any tomatoes anymore, because that was the thing he loved best to do, and he smiled for the first time, no, he said, no tomatoes. Then we went down the dusty road to the guard station and back and did it once again and the third time and still he did not want to sit. We tried to rest on a bench for a few minutes, but he got up and started off by himself, so we went with him. The men at the guard station said we could take him into town if we liked, so we decided we would try that out. There were two restaurants just up the road they said, so we thought maybe we could get him some lunch and buy him a carton of cigarettes.

We found this little family-style place—the sign in front said GOOD FOOD, and the menu had plate lunches with the standard meatloaf and pork chops and chicken-fried steak with gravy. But Daddy didn't want anything to eat, he just kept shaking his head when we asked, he just wanted his coffee and cigarettes. Donna and I had a hamburger, but we had to eat pretty quick because he was getting so nervous and needed to get out and walk some more. I knew the waitress must have thought something was wrong with Daddy, because his hands were shaking so around the coffee cup and he couldn't sit still, but she was patient, and didn't let on that she noticed anything at all. They probably get people from the hospital pretty often, I thought.

When we got back to the hospital, it was almost time to leave. Daddy had to go down for his nap and Donna and I were just about worn out by the visit. We walked him back to his room, and told him that we had to go, but he didn't want us to leave—he kept hanging on to my arm, and every time we said we really had to go and let him rest, he looked like he was going to cry, and then he said Sis, and reached into the top drawer of his bedside table and pulled it out, his old football picture, the one of Coach Wilbanks and the championship team.

I took the picture and looked at it and told him what a good picture it was, and how I wished I could have seen him play. And that was God's truth: if I could have my wish in the afterlife, well, I'd have two: I'd wish to see Jesus, I mean the man who told those hard stories, not the Jesus on the wall at Sunday School, and I'd wish to see my daddy play football like he did when he was young.

We moved to go then, and every step I took away from him, I felt more like a deserter. He was the one person who needed me as nobody else ever had. I could never have taken him with me, of course. I knew that I couldn't save him, that he had come to this, through reasons known and unknown, and he had to live out his life the best way he could, and I had to live out mine. What good are words in these times, I thought, and yet they were all I had. I turned back to hold him and to tell him once more, I love you, Daddy, don't forget that I love you, and left him looking after me like a lost child.

CHAPTER 54

in which I try to save a life

SEPARATED, BUT NOT YET DIVORCED, I CONTINUED TO LIVE IN LEXINGTON and studied to become a social worker at the University of Kentucky. I got my MSW just months before Ronald Reagan was elected President and social work programs began being cut all over the nation. Really bad timing. I got a job, lost it, got another, and lost it. Actually, I lost three jobs in two years. After living on unemployment checks for a few months, I found a fourth job as a program director at Alternatives for Women, an agency designed to help women stop medicating with drink or drugs after they lost their husbands or their jobs or both.

It was almost five o'clock one Monday afternoon, and I was getting ready to head for home, when I heard a mournful cry, followed by rustling, scratching noises in the wall, just to the right of my desk. A rat, maybe? suggested Alicia, the agency director. She called to Sarah, the secretary. We three women gathered round the spot, bending down to listen, our heads almost touching.

Silence, and then a flurry of movement and more cries. Silence, and more silence. Well, let's see if the creature—whatever it is—is still here tomorrow, said Alicia, raising her head. I'm ready to hang it up for today. We all agreed—let's see if the sounds are still there tomorrow.

The next morning we didn't hear anything. Well, I guess our rat found its way out, said Alicia. But around noon I heard it again. At first the sound was faint, but then louder, *scratch, scratch,* and then the same desperate cry. *This is no rat.* While the other two were at lunch, I put my ear to the wall and tried to figure out what manner of creature this was. I banged on the thin plasterboard wall, and the creature responded with louder cries and more scratching. *It's alive, and wants out.* Again I pounded on the wall, this time even harder.

I went outside the building to examine the outer wall. Looking up to the second floor where the agency's offices were, I noticed that the roof joined the top of the building at just about the spot where the creature was trapped. Birds were flying in to rest under the overhang, out of the heat of the day. *A bird, of course!*

When Alicia and Sarah came back, I told them my theory, and they agreed that yes, we had a bird in there. But what to do? Alicia said that maybe it would find its way out.

No, it hasn't yet, I said, and was unlikely to, in its weakened state.

We'll just have to let it die, she said, in her best businesslike voice. We don't have that kind of money, to go cutting open walls to get birds out.

No, of course the agency didn't have the money—and yet the bird's pathetic cries and scratching sounds kept recurring at intervals throughout the day. *How long can it last in there, without food or water?*

Once again I went home and busied myself with supper and the children. But the crying of the trapped bird haunted me the whole evening. *It's surely dying now, surely it will be gone by tomorrow morning.* It became almost unbearable to think about this fellow creature in the wall, cut off from its companions, in the darkness, languishing.

Waking before the break of day, I lay there as the sun gradually turned the dark room to gray and then to the rosy shade of the old-fashioned wallpaper in my bedroom. *Is the bird still alive?* I got the children ready and dropped them off at school earlier than usual, arriving at the office well before anyone else. As I turned the key in the lock and slipped in, I noticed how like a sanctuary the office was, the early morning sun streaming in golden strips through the eastern windows, the dust dancing in the light. Every-thing in the large room was borrowed or donated or makeshift, but there was a rightness to it that morning. I breathed deeply and took in the quiet.

I knelt on the floor and put my ear to the wall where the bird was trapped. I heard nothing. I knocked on the wall, but no response. I knocked louder, and still nothing. I began to panic, I had a conviction of guilt, a sure knowledge that what should have been done had not been done, and that the time to act had now passed. Again I knocked, this time hard, with the flat of my hand, against the side of the wall. *Scratch, scratch.* I barely heard it at first, I put my ear back to the wall. *Scratch, scratch.* This time it was louder. I hit the wall again, as hard as before, and the bird cried out, a loud raucous screech. I'm here! I yelled, before I thought. I'm going to get you out! Hang on!

It's still alive I said, as Alicia came through the door.

What?

The bird. It's still alive. We have to get it out.

Now wait a minute. How are we going to do that without spending money, we don't have money to spend on this kind of thing.

Look, I said, if this bird dies in there, we'll have to get it out anyway—it'll decay, and the smell will go all through this place. It'll be unbearable, for us and for the clients.

Alicia paused, thoughtfully. Good point, she said.

In truth, Alicia didn't want to see the bird die either. When Sarah came in a few minutes later, we consulted with her, and all three of us decided that yes, the bird should be freed. I called the maintenance man for the building, who came promptly, and sawed through the plasterboard as we three women stood around him, watching. I hardly dared to breathe, as if by not breathing, I could give air to the trapped creature. It was quiet. *Maybe it's dead already.* But no, when the small square opening was made, and the maintenance man reached in, we heard frantic movement and loud cries. He pulled out a scruffy bundle of black feathers with wild shiny eyes. Who wants it? he asked. We three women all looked at one another.

I'll take it, I said, and wiped my sweaty palms on my pants, before reaching out. I held the trembling creature tightly in both hands, feeling its heart pounding mightily. Somebody open the door!

I carried the bird down the stairs to the open courtyard at the rear of the building. The instant I released it, the bird took to the air. It was free! It circled round once and round again—and then headed straight for the brick building that housed the insurance agency next door. It flew headlong into the wall, and fell to a motionless heap on the ground.

I ran to the bird and picked it up out of the dirt and gravel. No longer struggling, its shiny black feathers covered with the gray dust, it lay still in my hands, its eyes closed, its small heart pumping frantically. *It wasn't ready to fly, how stupid of me!* I placed the bird in the shade under the steps to the agency, and went inside to get some water.

When I came back, I carefully lifted the bird and placed its beak in the cup of water. Its eyes opened, and it drank. I stroked the tiny black head. You're going to be all right. Drink your water. Then suddenly the bird's heart stopped, and its head flopped to one side. I stared at the inert form in my hands. I waited, hoping for a murmur, or the least little movement. I gave the black heap a gentle shake. But the tiny feet had already begun to curl up in death.

The bird visited my dreams for months to come: I heard the scratching and screeching that were its call for life. At work I saw the crudely patched wall, and I remembered the shiny fearful eyes of the creature as it was being taken from its prison. Again and again, I saw the black body smashing into the red brick wall and falling limp into the dust. *Smashing and falling. Smashing and falling.* The reaching for the water, the pounding of the heart, straining beyond itself. Then the curling of the tiny claws. I did my best, but I failed. It just wasn't ready to fly.

CHAPTER 55

in which my heart is torn

I WOKE UP HUMMING "YOU ARE MY SUNSHINE." I WONDERED AT THIS. I smiled at myself and shook my head. Why "You Are My Sunshine," and why for god's sake in the morning? I pulled on my jeans and sweatshirt and headed for the boys' room. Wake up, Pooks! Time for school! When they groused, I began singing to them, with gusto: You are my sunshine, my only sunshine, you make me happy when skies are blue. You'll never know, Dear . . .

The boys covered their ears and squealed, Stop it, Mommy! Stop, stop! and crawled more deeply into the bedclothes. I pulled them out, first Kash and then Madison. Both curly heads, just like Frank. I dressed them for their preschool, pulling undershirts and cotton turtlenecks over their sleepy eyes. I continued humming under my breath: Please don't take my sunshine away.

After the children were picked up, I lingered at the breakfast table with my big red mug full of coffee. I had made myself a second cup, although I didn't really know if I wanted it. I wasn't sure what I *did* want. Maybe I should work on that feature story for the newspaper, I thought. No, maybe later. The possibility of sweet-smelling bread entered my imagination, and before I knew it, I got up to see if I had some yeast. *It's all here, yes. I want the bread today.* I got out my crockery mixing bowl, the old cream-colored one I got at the flea market years ago, and began measuring and mixing. I put the mixture aside to rise.

A couple of hours later I poured the warm puffy dough out on my largest breadboard. I began pushing it under the heels of my hands, turning and pushing, again and again, my nostrils filling with the sweet yeasty smell. *It's almost breathing.* I worked it and worked it, feeling for the elasticity that would tell me that the dough was ready to be formed into loaves. *Yes, now. Into the oven.*

Without bothering to get a sweater, I walked out the back-door. The maple tree had never been more beautiful. Brilliant reds, oranges, yellows mingled against a cold blue sky, the ground all around the tree was blanketed with the fallen leaves. I sighed, and breathed deeply. A sharpness in the air caught in my throat. For a moment my mind stopped its incessant whirring, and thanksgiving rose unexpectedly within me—thanksgiving for the beauty of the day, the clean chill of the air, and the warmth of my kitchen, where my bread was now rising. *Dear tree, dear leaves, dear sky.*

I would have stayed longer but for the cold. Wrapping my arms around myself, I took one last look at the tree and the sky, and turned again to the haven that was my kitchen. I loved the house, built so long ago. I liked to think of the families who had sat down to meals here. For a hundred years children had been fed, people had said thanks, quarrels had been mended in this kitchen. *For a hundred years.* Well, I said aloud, and patted the table. Well.

The doorbell rang. It was only the postman, asking me for postage due on a rather fat envelope. I ran to get the money, and as he handed me the mail, he smiled and said, Fresh bread. Um-uh! Does that smell good! He turned to continue on his rounds. Nice day, isn't it?

Beautiful, I said. I closed the large wooden door against the cold, and turned the lock. I put the bulk of the mail down on the hall table, and then looked curiously at the envelope that had cost me eleven cents. "Mettinger, Lawson, and Hass." Frank's lawyer was Lawson. Really, *our* lawyer—he was handling the divorce for both of us. I tapped the envelope on my palm. I held it out from me and felt its weight. Thick, fine paper. First quality. I noted the light playing through the blue and gold stained glass window that arched its color over the hall. It was always lovely in the mornings. *No, it's too soon.* I decided to open the envelope.

I see the divorce papers, my name signed there, and Frank's name, and both names were the same last name. I see the signature of the judge, making the divorce legal. Though I have asked for this, parts of me never wanted it, wanted instead to be content, wanted to love this man and stay with him. *One day I'll have a family*, I had promised myself, all through my childhood.

I am stunned. I feel like somebody who has been casually contemplating suicide and then who accidentally steps off the edge of a precipice, surprised to be falling through space.

I lower myself to the floor in the large entrance hall and sit cross-legged on the thick blue carpet, directly under the glass chandelier. It is still moving and tinkling with the play of the wind, which had come in through the opened door. I sit staring at the papers in my hands, and the blue of the carpet is like the blue of the ocean, and the walls recede all around me, and I feel as though I am floating, supported only by the uncertain waves of this blue sea.

A strange buzzing sound begins to break in. A harsh sound. What can it be? I smell the bread baking—ready now, the stove is warning me—and I rise and walk, still dazed to the kitchen. Perfect bread, I say, as I pull the loaves from the oven. I look out the window at the maple. I take off the oven mitts and hold their warmth to my body, then to my face.

The bread is too hot to cut, but I cut it anyway. I get the serrated knife and slice a good inch and a half off one end of the loaf, then spread it with butter, and watch the butter melt. I raise the bread to my lips, and as I bite into it, my tears begin to fall, and they fall as if they will never stop, and even as I eat this good bread and taste its goodness, I also taste the salty bitterness of my tears.

You've done it now, I say out loud. You've really done it.

CHAPTER 56

in which I grieve what is gone

FRANK WAS GONE, BUT THE MARRIAGE KEPT GOING ON AND ON, THE WAY marriages will do. There's the tool set he insisted on buying and never used. His old t-shirt that I used to polish shoes. The dress shirt he left, the one with blue stripes that I hate to iron and always leave at the bottom of the "to iron" stack.

Somebody's spirit gets in a house and just stays, even after the person's long gone.

I knew I needed to move on to whatever I was moving on to. I thought it would help if I sold some things. Besides, I needed the money. First I sold the Volvo station wagon. That wasn't a hard decision. It was a lemon, anyway—the wipers kept stopping on me, an inconvenience when I was driving sixty miles an hour down the highway in a rainstorm. I got a good price, and bought an ancient Oldsmobile, like Daddy used to drive. Much better for me. No prestige, of course, but I had given that up with the marriage. As a doctor's wife, I could get credit anywhere, for anything. Banks almost beg doctors to take out a loan. As a divorced woman, though, I couldn't get a credit card. This was before the days when credit card companies were encouraging eighteen-year-old college students with no income to sign up for one.

I started selling the rest of the antiques–at least all the good stuff. I had too much furniture, anyway. I had already sold the Regency dining room table and the Chippendale chairs and the inlaid china cabinet to make room for the disco. Next I sold the

18th century slant front desk. And I sold the Georgian grandfather clock I had bought in London. When Frank told me he was going to remarry, I knew I'd better sell that clock, or he'd take it. Or she would. I felt bad about selling it, after the fact, though. It was his clock, really. I had bought it for him, and I wanted him to have it. But I couldn't stand the idea of his having it in another house, with another woman. So I called up a dealer I knew and said, how much for the clock, it's the best piece I've got. He gave me half what I paid for it and I was lucky at that. It was a beauty.

For years I had an on-going fantasy about the clock. *One day I'll have money again. I'm looking in an antique shop one day, and I see a clock just like Frank's. It might even be Frank's. Who knows. I buy this clock and have it delivered to his address, without telling him anything ahead of time. He's much older now, maybe twenty or thirty years older, and the last thing he's expecting is a clock from me. He says to the delivery man, I didn't order a clock, and the man says it's a gift, and confirms the name on the delivery order, and gets Frank, who is totally baffled, to sign. On the back of the clock is taped a sealed envelope. Frank opens it, and recognizes my handwriting immediately. Here's your clock, Honey. I didn't mean to take it from you. Frank is overwhelmed. He remembers me, what we had together. He sets up the clock, and gets it ticking. He never lets it stop.*

During the next financial crisis, I decided to sell my engagement ring and my wedding band, locked together as they were, and my gold bracelet, the one Frank had given me on our first anniversary. The diamond itself was such a good one, nearly flawless, that the jeweler who bought it thought at first it might be fake, but when he took a closer look, he said that it was almost perfect, which is what I told him from the beginning. Almost perfect. That's what Frank wanted for me. And the gold bracelet, too, was of finest quality. The best.

I was amazed at how much money I got from this jeweler, who was somewhat on the sleazy side. I'm sure it wasn't nearly what Frank had paid. Of course, it wouldn't be. When I walked out of the store the light caught me, I had to turn away. It made my eyes water. When my eyes adjusted after a few minutes, I looked down at my left hand, and it seemed naked. Now I hadn't worn my rings for over a year, so I don't know why I reacted that way, but I did. Maybe it was because I knew I could never put those rings back on again. Not that I wanted to. But I hate to say "never." You never know, is what I say. Realistically, though, was Frank going to change into another man? No, he was just going to keep on being Frank. I told myself, get real, get through the "grieving process" and get on with your life, I told myself. But it didn't happen that way. I wanted the rings back, and the bracelet. Frank gave them to me because he loved me the best way he knew how, and I went and sold them to this fat, pock-faced jeweler down south of Main Street.

There's no honor there.

So what if you had kept them, I said to myself. What in the world would you do with them? And I answered myself, a stone can be reset. Or a ring can become a pin. Metamorphosis is possible, isn't it?

CHAPTER 57

in which I give myself over

When the alarm rang at 4:15 a.m., my body lay like a tree felled in the forest, a tree felled so long ago that the memory of standing was gone. But there was no question of staying in bed—I was doing an early morning advice show, *Dear Mary Catherine*, for WKYT television and my fans were expecting me. All over central Kentucky people would be stretching with the morning light and waiting to hear what Mary Catherine had to say about their bad marriages or their impossible boss or their best friend who had betrayed them. At least that was my fantasy. I couldn't just call in sick because I was tired. Everybody gets tired, for god's sake.

I drove out to the station in a kind of daze, keeping the radio on high, to keep me alert. Once the show starts, I will be all right, I thought. I always come through.

But I wasn't all right. When I looked into the camera and tried to remember what it was I wanted to say, I kept going blank, kept having to look down at my script. Every time I looked up again the brightness seemed to half blind me, and I saw dark spots floating round the camera face, and spikes of light. *If I could only sleep . . .*

At last the show was over. I crawled into my ancient and gargantuan Oldsmobile, folded my arms over the steering wheel and rested my head for a few minutes, then cranked up the engine and started home. I felt safe in the Olds. It was so big and had been dented so often that other drivers avoided me—that car took no prisoners. I thought maybe I'd get some coffee before work started at eight.

⁂

I hear the sound of my own voice calling out the names of my children. Kash, Madison, Kash, Madison, over and over again. I am not fully awake, but I know something bad has happened. I hear the whine of the siren, feel the turning and bouncing of the vehicle I am in, see the white coats bending over me, trying to wake me up, smell something sharp under my nose. I turn my face away. Marilyn, Marilyn, wake up! says an urgent male voice. A hand is gently slap, slap, slapping one side of my face. Wake up!

When I wake the second time, I am on a table in a large white room. My friend Barbara is holding my hand, and people in green gowns are looking down at me. She's coming to, someone says, and the green gowns draw closer. Their voices come together in a warm murmur as they watch me. I hear but cannot move, cannot answer. I lie on their table and let them fuss over me. Barbara's cool hand is stroking my wrist.

It seems that I had passed out while driving back from the show, going 60 miles per hour. When my foot left the accelerator, the car ran off the road and meandered into a filling station, crashing ever so gently into a parked car. Someone had called an ambulance. Mercifully, I was unhurt—my angel must have been watching over me. Nobody knew why I was unconscious, so they kept me on the emergency room table for observation, where shortly they observed me having a seizure. They figured that's what had happened on the road.

I stayed in the hospital eight days and was given every kind of test you can imagine. I had no family history of seizures, so the doctors didn't know what to think, but when I began talking about all that was going on in my life—about the murder and my two jobs and the house and the children and money troubles and my back pain—they decided that I had had a "stress seizure," which happens to people sometimes when they push themselves too hard or when life is pushing them too hard. I expect it was a little of both for me. The body's natural solution to pressure, the doctor said, smiling.

Being in the hospital was a revelation of sorts. Lots of people called and came to see me—all manner of people I never knew even cared about me. I got flowers and cards and gifts until I couldn't help but understand that I was loved, and for nothing, I mean for nothing that I did for these people, just for being alive and being who I was. My sister Donna flew up from Alabama to be with me and take care of Kash and Madison. Frank didn't call or come to see me. I heard that he called my doctor to check on my condition. But he never talked to me. I think he wouldn't have known what to say.

The doctor sent me home after the week of testing. Rest, he said. Rest for at least a month. Then we'll see.

Day after day I lay there, almost in a stupor. Each moment belonged to itself alone, and I might do nothing more than notice the pattern on the quilt covering me, for hours. Time was all of a piece: I could distinguish no movement of the clock, except by the meal trays brought in. A spider was weaving her web in the corner next to my bed, sliding, climbing, pulling, tying. How curious. I wondered at her industry. I turned away from food. I couldn't imagine ever again laughing or talking or reading books or going to movies. I knew that I could be dead and maybe should have felt lucky for being alive, but I couldn't understand why I would want to be alive.

Then one day Granny came and sat with me. I don't know whether I was awake or dreaming when she came. She had been dead for almost twenty years.

Granny is in her easy chair, the big blue one, rocking in front of the fire like she always does, reading her old black Bible, the King James version with the big print, the red edges worn white in spots, as white as her hair. She is licking her finger and turning the page. She stops and reads: "Bless the Lord, O my soul, all that is within me, bless His holy name."

Lying there in my sick bed, I heard her say it as clear as day. How many times had I heard her read that same passage when I was growing up: Bless the Lord, O my soul, all that is within me, bless His holy name.

What would it mean for *all that is within me* to bless the name of God?

All that is within me. I didn't know what God was, but I had a good idea that it wasn't me. I was bone-tired, dog-weary of trying to control things. I thought I would rest, and just *be* for a while, and listen. I slept, and I dreamed.

The Junior League is giving a bazaar. Bring your clothes to be cleaned, they said, bring your best garments, the service is good, though the cost is high. I go to pick up my freshly cleaned garments and find they are hanging in trees, and I must find them myself. These clothes are still soiled, I say, and they say no, the clothes are perfect. I go to the woman in charge, and throw her to the ground choking her, trying to kill her. Her friends pull me off. Take your clothes and go, they are perfect, they say.

Daddy is chasing me through an old neighborhood, much like the one where my house stands—wide streets, trees looming down over stately Victorians. He has a gun. He is drinking, and he wants to kill me. I run from house to house, hiding in the shadows, behind posts, in cupboards, frantic, and he follows, but he cannot catch me because I know my way, I know where the safe places are and when to stop and when to move. He can never catch me, he can never kill me.

I have a baby, but not a whole baby, only the baby's head, which I keep well groomed and stored in the refrigerator. I take the whole family— Daddy, Brother, Sister, Baby—for a ride in the big blue Oldsmobile, which has two open holes in the rear, one with a rag stuck in. I go to a small village, where I lose my way. I can hardly drive for Daddy's big leg wrapped around my right leg. I have to go, I tell him, I have to get the baby home, move your leg or I'll cut it off.

I go to see the King of the Land, whose every wish is carried out. I have on a long dress, I am full-bosomed, with a tiny waist, full-rounded hips, and wide, innocent eyes. The King asks to sleep with me that night, and I am given over. The next morning he is distressed: I need you, I need you, he says over and over again, he is so furious at his need for me that he cuts me in four pieces, quarters me down and across. He pulls back the skin and muscles, revealing the viscera.

I am in my psychiatrist's bed, nude, and he says he needs to examine me. Full of passion and longing, soon he is nude, too. We are so very pleased to be this close, and we begin touching each other, exploring the textures and shapes of each other's body. Both of us are filled with delight, and make soft sounds of pleasure with the newness of it all. We are gentle, each wanting to please the other. Then he is gone, and I am back in the hospital. A nurse brings me a letter from him, which has been opened by one of the candy stripers. I am angry at first, but when I see his handwriting, I understand that only I can read it. He says that he has gone away to a place where he and his work will be appreciated. He says he has found the perfect woman for him there, she is a priest and also a cheerleader. He says that he is including a picture of her in the letter, and when I look, I find the photo of an owl. My supper is ready, the nurse says, and she serves me a large plate of carrots, which I eat with great relish.

These dreams went on for several weeks, and over time I gradually got my strength back and took an interest in the world outside my bed. I was changing, being restored. It was like when you've been working in the garden all day and you're filthy down to the fingernails and your head is itching because your hair needed washing two days ago and you go in and take a long shower, as long as you want, and wash your whole self clean again. You smell new, almost like a baby, and you touch your skin and it feels silky, and you want to be with folks again.

Or it's like you've been climbing all day up a rugged mountain trail, struggling through vines and brambles, tripping over roots and getting your shoes muddy, your tongue heavy and dry. Finally you stop a minute to rest and breathe and you turn and look back and the whole green valley and the river are laid out before you and you are a part of a wholeness that you never knew was there.

All that is within me. Don't ask me who God is. I still can't tell you. And another thing. I'm still alone in the world, and I know it. We all are.

After I got better, I was still scared and still didn't even know what was scaring me half the time. So I was alone, but I was not alone in the same way I used to be. I got down on my knees one day, literally on my knees, and I said outloud: I don't know whether or not you exist, God, but I'm here to say that I no longer belong to myself. I'm giving myself away, giving myself to the good, in whatever way it's shown to me. From this day on.

The Baptist minister used to say, You're bought with a price. He was talking about Jesus, I know, talking about Jesus's bloody death on the cross. But it was Granny who bought me—Granny and my mother. Before I was even born, don't you know. Southern Baptist and Catholic. But the labels don't nearly say it. These women both knew God. They were both given over. And here I am at last, by the hardest, given over. *All that is within me.*

꽃

CHAPTER 58

in which the Holy Spirit comes down like a dove . . . or maybe a sparrow

I HAD WORK AT THE WOMEN'S AGENCY AND ALSO THE PART-TIME TV JOB, but I couldn't make ends meet. I went to a financial advisor. She told me, It's not that you don't manage your money well, it's that you don't have enough money.

It was time for Plan B. I thought about getting a Ph.D. in education or perhaps in social work. I traveled up to Smith College to check out their social work program, and then the program at Brandeis, but neither seemed to fit. The minister at the Unitarian Universalist church in Lexington, Roger Fritts, had studied at Starr King School for the Ministry, a Unitarian Universalist seminary in Berkeley, California. He told me all about it—it sounded like an extraordinary institution. I was intrigued. Maybe I should consider seminary, I thought. I had always been religious, after all.

So I flew out to California for the first time in my life, flew into that strange land called Berkeley to interview at Starr King. I remember the interview well. One lay member of the committee asked me, What will you do if we don't accept you? I said, I don't know. Then in another interview, a professor asked me, What is your goal in life? I blurted out, I want to be all used up. He said, Well, parish ministry should do that for you.

Before I left Berkeley, the school told me I had been accepted. But should I go?

Deeply conflicted, I flew back home to think it over. I wasn't sure I wanted to become a parish minister. I knew only that I needed to make a living somehow and in some way be useful to others. My decision to go would mean leaving my boys in Kentucky with their father, who had established himself as a surgeon and had remarried. He was a good man and a good father who wanted to be with his sons. In a couple of years, Kash and Madison would be junior high age and needed to be with their father, rather than with a mother struggling to find herself. They needed stability. I knew all this. But rational thought did not assuage my hurt at the thought of leaving them.

❧

One morning about two weeks after I returned home, I was awakened before dawn. Something, some internal voice, told me to get dressed and go for a walk. Getting up at that hour is not something I would ever, ever consider doing of my own free will. Generally, I go to bed late, I get up late, and as yet I have never seen a sunrise unless forced to by some early plane I had to catch. But I knew I must obey this voice.

I got up, put on my jeans and my jacket, and walked out into the dark. I walked without a destination in mind, just one step after the next, and ended up at Transylvania, a nearby university.*

The campus was a broad expanse of green with one smallish tree in sight. I walked toward the tree, the darkness giving way to light, and I saw there amongst the branches a little brown bird. I moved closer and closer to the tree and to the bird, in the eerie silence of the early morning, until I was standing right next to the bird. Strangely, *it did not fly away.* I stayed there with the bird for

---

* I missed the significance of that name at the time. Transylvania is where our Unitarian faith began in Europe centuries ago, in the country now known as Romania.

a few minutes, and then I walked back home. Without thinking— just moving automatically—I got out my old Remington portable typewriter and typed out my acceptance letter to Starr King.

Now what was this all about? I don't know. All I can do is report my experience. Much later in seminary when I was casually thumbing through a dictionary of religious symbols one day, it hit me—of course! The bird is the traditional symbol of the Spirit. I remembered the dove descending when Jesus was baptized, I remembered the dove that told Noah land was near. My little bird was not so dramatic or so imposing – just a little sparrow, most likely, hovering in the dark and waiting for the dawn.

Years later I recounted this experience to my son Madison during a road trip we were taking together. He was in college at the time studying mathematics, physics, and logic, so I was a bit reluctant to tell the story, anticipating that he might be skeptical. When I finished the telling, I paused dramatically and waited. He said, Mom, that's the stupidest thing I've ever heard.

Well, maybe so, but I staked my life on it. Several months after my encounter with the bird, I left for Berkeley with a suitcase and two boxes of books.

CHAPTER 59

in which I witness evil

I WAS IN A MOOD. I DECIDED ON A WALK TO THE LEXINGTON CITY CEME-tery. It was full of flowering trees and shrubs—pink, purple, white—and surrounded by a grove of tall, dignified trees. It was a lovely place, as cemeteries go. A place for walking and thinking.

I wandered amidst the gravestones, reading the inscriptions: names like Clarence Walker, Denise Walker; Roger Rutherford and His Beloved Wife Evelyn; Kathryn McFarland, Joseph McFarland, Son Christopher, May They Rest in Peace. All families—husbands, wives, children—together in life, together in death. I suddenly grew tired and sat down on one of the wooden benches to rest. Should I go to California, or not? How can I leave the boys? How can I leave my heart? Just at that moment I heard what sounded like a series of gunshots.

As I approached the viaduct on my way back, through decidedly not the best part of town, I saw two policemen putting their pistols back in their holsters and laughing and pointing to something in the dry gully below. I walked within a few yards of them and looked down over the rail. Below me was a mother possum nosing the dead bodies of her eight young, all of which apparently had been shot by the two policemen. What happened? I asked. At first they seemed not to hear, they kept on laughing and joshing, each elbowing the other playfully. I spoke more loudly, What happened here?

The little lady wants to know what happened here, Sam. Why don't you tell her.

Why don't you tell her, said the other.

No, you.

No, you. They both were overcome with laughter.

Well, nothing really happened. Just a little target practice, that's all. Sam here had to admit that I'm a better shot. And once again the shorter of the two elbowed the other and guffawed.

You killed these possums? I asked. For no good reason, you shot all the babies?

Well, let me ask you something, said the taller one with the close-cropped blond hair. What good is a possum? Used to be, the niggers would eat them, but now even they won't. What good is a possum?

Look at the mother, I said, pointing in the gully at the mother still trying to nose her babies into life. Why didn't you just kill her, too? How do you think she feels without her babies?

How does a possum *feel*? I don't know—Jerry, how does a possum feel? Both men doubled over in laughter at the notion.

Sam spoke next. Maybe the little lady is right. Maybe we should kill the big one, too. He made as if to reach for his gun, to see what I would say next.

If you touch that gun, I'm going to have your ass in court, I said. I had no idea if I could do that or not. What are your names?

Seeing as how you want to put us in jail for killing possums, I don't reckon I for one want to give you my name, Honey. They stopped laughing.

You're disgusting, both of you. And in uniform, you did this. I'll get your names, don't worry.

I turned and walked at a quick pace to my house, where I telephoned the police station. It was not much, I thought, but I had to do something.

The image haunted me for months, though: the mother possum waddling and whining and pushing her nose at her bloody young, wanting to give them life again. *What's a possum good for?*

CHAPTER 60

in which I leave my children

KASH AND MADISON WERE TO STAY WITH THEIR FATHER WHILE I WAS IN seminary. Frank had a surgery practice in Henderson, Kentucky. He had a good income, a new wife, a church, a place in the world. I didn't have money, or a job, or even a place to live. He readily agreed to this arrangement, and also promised to pay their way to California for Christmas each year, and to send them to me for their summer vacation.

I arranged my flight. I had two more weeks in Lexington, two more weeks with my sons.

The boys and I had a bedtime ritual—it was the best time of my day. They would cry, Read a story, Mommy! Read a story!

Reluctantly, I settle into E.B. White's *Charlotte's Web,* and soon the beauty and peace of the book draw me in. The children sit on either side of me, on Kash's bed, snuggling close. I feel the pressure and ache in my chest ease a bit. Well, where are we? Just about to the end, I guess. Wilbur is talking to Charlotte.

> "Charlotte," said Wilbur. "We're all going home today. The Fair is almost over. Won't it be wonderful to be back home in the barn cellar again with the sheep and the geese? Aren't you anxious to get home?"
>
> For a moment Charlotte said nothing. Then she spoke in a voice so low Wilbur could hardly hear the words.
>
> "I will not be going back to the barn," she said.

Wilbur leapt to his feet. "Not going back?" he cried. "Charlotte, what are you talking about?"

"I'm done for," she replied. "In a day or two I'll be dead. I haven't even strength enough to climb down into the crate. I doubt if I have enough silk in my spinnerets to lower me to the ground."

Hearing this, Wilbur threw himself down in an agony of pain and sorrow. Great sobs racked his body. He heaved and grunted with desolation. "Charlotte," he moaned. "Charlotte! My true friend!"

I read on, trying to ignore the tears that begin to slip from my eyes. I don't want the children to know that I am crying, but the tears fall on my hands and onto the pages of the book. I keep reading in an even, compassionate voice.

Mommy, don't cry, Madison says, and he puts his thin arms around me and asks me again, Please don't cry. I know that I have gone too far. I never intended to cry in front of them tonight, I did that last week, that's no good for kids, they're scared if their mom cries.

So I put it off on E. B. White and say, This story is sad, boys, and that's why I'm crying. It's all right to cry when the story is sad, isn't it, that's what I've always said, haven't I? And they halfway believe me and sit closer. I wipe my eyes on the sleeve of my old gray sweatshirt and the words on the page clear up and my body warms and eases as I continue to read, and I am suddenly profoundly thankful that these two particular children were born to me, and I think myself a most fortunate woman. I laugh out loud at a funny part, and the boys laugh, too. I exaggerate the characters' voices, and the boys giggle, and they beg, Read some more, read some more!

Well, just five more pages, I say and begin again and when that's over I say, OK, no more. Time for bed, you have school tomorrow, you know.

No, no! they protest in unison. But they obey.

I tuck each boy in and ask each in turn what he feels thankful for. Kash says he's tired of being thankful every night and says he wants to say his own prayers to himself and sometimes anyway he doesn't feel thankful and so why should he say he is. I smile and say OK, fine, whatever you want, night-night, I love you, Honey. And he hugs me for a long time.

Madison says he's thankful for Granddaddy and Nonnie and for Uncle Tom and Aunt Martha Ann and Carmie and Susan and Christopher and Aunt Donna and Uncle Jim, and Daddy, and . . . Mommy's boobies! He laughs hysterically at this, his favorite bedtime joke, which he stumbled upon years before. I laugh and tickle him until he says, Stop, stop, I won't ever say it again, promise! promise!

I stop and pull the blankets up over him and make sure that Mother Goose and Raggedy Ann and Baby Kuola all have cover. I love you a hundred, he says.

I love you a thousand, I answer. And we each try to outdo the other, as usual.

A million.

A billion.

A hundred billion.

A hundred million billion.

A trillion.

A hundred million billion trillion.

I love you infinigy! he says at last.

Me, too, I say, new tears rushing to my eyes. I love you infinigy, too, Honey. Night-night.

CHAPTER 61

in which I am told, Yes!

WHEN A DIRECTION IS RIGHT, ALL THE PIECES SEEM TO FALL INTO PLACE. Upon arriving in Berkeley, I found everything I needed. I found a rent-controlled apartment up the hill from Starr King, in a grove of eucalyptus trees. Deer sometimes strolled in the parking lot. I found a companion, a graduate student from Taiwan, who loaned me his old Ford Pinto, cooked noodles with black bean sauce for me, and invited me into his bed. He was ten years younger and wanted children of his own one day. That suited me--I wanted a lover and a friend, but not a husband. Insofar as our differences would admit, we loved each other.

Most important, I found a school whose philosophy is to say "Yes!" to students.

Starr King School for the Ministry is a unique institution. It is named after Thomas Starr King, the young Universalist minister of the First Unitarian Church of San Francisco, who is credited with saving California for the Union with his brilliant oratory. Starr King is part of the Graduate Theological Union, a consortium of nine member schools of various faiths. Students can take classes from any of those seminaries and can also choose from the vast offerings of the nearby University of California at Berkeley.

The school was founded on the assumption that students are adults who know what they need, so in consultation with their advisors, students choose their own classes. After finishing degrees in three conventional schools—a BA in English Education at

Louisiana Polytechnic, an MA in English Literature from the University of Arkansas, and a Masters in Social Work (MSW) from the University of Kentucky—matriculating at Starr King was like being in an academic candy store for me. I gobbled up everything that attracted me, while being sure that I was preparing myself adequately for the parish. Gandhi? Black preaching? Creative writing? Tillich? All these, along with the usual church history, religious education, and denominational polity.

To say that I flourished under the positive philosophy of the school is a vast understatement. Starr King was made for someone like me. It opened the way not only for my professional development, but for my personal development as well, giving me a growing confidence that I had something good to offer.

I met Albert Chen, my Taiwanese friend, the second day I arrived in Berkeley. I was having lunch alone in a Chinese restaurant on Euclid, and he was at the table beside me. He smiled and said, You use your chopsticks well! It's as good an opening line as any. Albert was not his birth name of course. He said he chose that because of his admiration for Albert Einstein, only to discover once he arrived here that Albert was kind of a dorky name. It stuck, though.

We were together for most of the time I was in Berkeley—during my last two years, he moved to Japan for work in the financial industry. I had never known anyone from Taiwan—or Japan or China, for that matter—and I had never dated a person of color. I learned about a different culture, and I learned also about prejudice. For example, I watched people being condescending to Albert because his English was not perfect. Though our coupling was not designed to last forever, our relationship was marked by great affection. It was right for both of us at the time.

All during that first year of seminary, I grieved terribly the loss of my sons. Many a night Albert held me while I cried myself to sleep. Playful and high-spirited, he became a friend to my boys. They took to him immediately—especially after that first Christmas, when he showered them with gifts. All during my Berkeley years, eight in all, the boys spent Christmases and summers with Albert and me.

After my parish internship at First Unitarian in Dallas, Texas, with John Buehrens, who subsequently became President of the Unitarian Universalist Association, I went back to Starr King for a fourth and final year to finish my Masters of Divinity. But by then I had realized that I wanted to do a Ph.D. I was taking a creative writing class with Ron Loewinsohn, novelist and critic at the University of California. When I mentioned I was considering the Ph.D., he volunteered to be my dissertation director—his offer was hugely significant, since my emphasis was theology and literature. I had studied preaching with Edwina Hunter of Pacific School of Religion, and she was on board as a member of my committee. Claire Fischer, a scholar and feminist who was a professor at Starr King, completed the committee. Claire knew the push and pull of the doctoral process quite well, and with her guidance, I finished the degree in four years of additional study.

My son Madison came to spend his last two years of high school in Berkeley. Having him with me brought great joy after the protracted separation from my children. He and I had long conversations over dinner most nights. I watched him struggle in the new school environment and finally flourish. He and I graduated together in 1991. My first book, *Cries of the Spirit*, an anthology of spiritual poetry by women, was the first of its kind. It was based on research I did for the doctorate and was published by Beacon Press the same year I finished school.

I had very little money during these eight years—I remember wearing the same old tan corduroy pants and jacket every day. I worked stuffing envelopes for the Development Department of Starr King, and I was the consulting minister at a small Unitarian Universalist church in Vallejo—being paid $6,000 a year for quarter-time work, but actually working half time.

I knew by heart the price of every item in the grocery store, and if bananas went up ten cents a pound, I didn't buy them. I allowed myself the guilty pleasure of an occasional cup of cappuccino at Peet's Coffee. Madison, to his father's dismay, was on the free lunch program at Berkeley High, but it was a superb school in which he was nourished intellectually and socially. I felt rich in all the ways that matter.

This was perhaps the happiest period of my life. Learning has always been a deep pleasure for me, and I had the serenity and security that comes from being absolutely in place, with little of the stress that comes from a demanding job.

I didn't know what exactly I would do after graduation. I figured I could be a writer, an academic, or a parish minister. Soon my prospects narrowed—I couldn't make a living being a writer, and there were virtually no job openings in the academy for theology and the arts. Should I become a minister, then? The way, I hoped, would be made clear.

CHAPTER 62

in which I search for my call, in vain

I DECIDED TO LOOK FOR A POSITION AS A PARISH MINISTER. HOWEVER, MY search for a church pulpit did not go well. In our denomination, the search process is long and elaborate. The search committee chooses somewhere between two and five "pre-candidates" to interview. Typically, the pre-candidating minister arrives on a Friday, is shown around town, and then enters a grueling three days of information gathering and meetings with the committee. On Sunday the minister preaches in a neutral pulpit, has lunch with the committee, and leaves for home. When all the pre-candidating is done, the committee chooses one of the ministers to "candidate," or be presented by the search committee to the congregation for a weeklong visit, preaching on the Sunday before and after, and then standing for a vote from the full congregation.

Most ministers do two, maybe three pre-candidatings in order to find a church. The final year of my doctoral studies, I did five pre-candidatings all over the country, from Florida to California, but no church seemed right for me. The head of the UU Placement Department was irritated. He told me that I was "being aloof" with these churches. I told him I did not feel called.

I believed, and still believe, that ministers should feel called to a church before accepting a position. Finding the right match is crucial, and good ministers can fail if they allow themselves to take a church for the wrong reasons. It's always tempting to choose a position because of the sunshine or because you have friends or family in the area. And a generous salary can turn a minister's head. But the call doesn't have to do with size or location of the church, or with salary. It doesn't have to do with the minister's need for a job, or conversely, with the church's pressing need for a minister. It is a love affair that is ignited during pre-candidating. I had not fallen in love. I had not been called.

On the other hand, I had student debt, and I needed work. I asked the Department of Ministry if I could do an interim ministry for a year. The Department agreed, and I began receiving slips of paper in the mail, letting me know of available interims. I kept throwing them in the trash. *What is wrong with me?*

Then one day a slip came suggesting the First Unitarian Church in Cincinnati. It was as though my angel had come down and touched me with the message I had been looking for: I knew instantly that I must go to Cincinnati. Without thinking, I called up the head of the interim search committee and said I wanted to take the position. I refrained from telling her that God sent me. Surprised at my assertiveness, she told me they were just starting to look at candidates. She asked me to send my packet, and they would let me know in a month or two. As I suspected, God got it right, and I was chosen.

Cincinnati was, of course, the city where our family was living when Daddy took us children so abruptly from our mother. I didn't make the psychological connection at first—I couldn't articulate exactly why I felt compelled to go to Cincinnati—but once again, an internal necessity drove my decision. Once there, I realized that I was not ready for a call as yet: I needed to explore the loss of my mother.

I secured a psychiatrist, Madelyn, to help me with this work and saw her weekly for nine months or so. One day I brought in some artwork I had done. It was abstract, all in slashing red streaks. What does red mean to you? she asked.

Love, I said. Passion, maybe.

What about anger? she said. *Yes, what about anger.* To avoid visiting that anger on some congregation, I needed to acknowledge it in myself. To look at the source. To see what was supporting my drifts into depression.

For much of that year, I struggled emotionally. The psychological work was demanding. But I was very much alive and present, and the church was a healthy one with strong lay leadership, so my ministry flourished. I continued searching, doing four more pre-candidatings. I was becoming very good at interviewing, so churches wanted me. But I did not want them. *Why was nothing working out?* I began questioning whether or not I was supposed to be a minister at all. Then First Unitarian Church in Portland, Oregon, asked me to pre-candidate. This was the tenth and last church I looked at.

I wasn't supposed to be on the Unitarian Universalist Association's (UUA's) list for First Unitarian in Portland —it was a large church of around 675 members, and I was just out of seminary, having never served a church as their called minister. The UUA's recommended list for the Portland church was filled with men, so in the Placement Department's wish to be egalitarian and inclusive, they wanted at least one female. I was a female with a Ph.D., so bingo! *Was this the church I had been looking for?*

CHAPTER 63

in which I find my call

I HAD NEVER BEEN TO PORTLAND—OR TO THE NORTHWEST, FOR THAT matter. As my plane neared the ground, I was captured by the bold landscape, with its mountains and towering trees. I found it daunting and, at the same time, compelling. My love affair was beginning.

I was met at the airport by two members of the search committee and driven around the city to look at typical neighborhoods, with their lush gardens and tree-lined streets, which I found most charming. Then I was taken to the church. Though it is the fourth incarnation of the church, the present building is a classic New England structure, reflecting the heritage of the founders, prominent individuals from the East who established the church in 1866. Unlike most of our Unitarian Universalist churches, it has a steeple. The structure of the building says something about respect for tradition and, with its raised pulpit, respect for ministry, as well. It is an elegant structure and beautifully appointed. First Unitarian is an urban church, located in the heart of downtown Portland. Since its founding, the institution had been a significant force for good in the community.

When I left the sanctuary that day, I knew I wanted to worship in that beauty, and I wanted to be a part of that tradition. Would the search committee agree?

The first meeting with the committee was in the home of a woman who lived in Eastmoreland, an area mostly of cottages built in the 1920s and '30s. The season was spring, and yards were awash in color: rhododendrons, azaleas, tulips, daffodils. The home was near Reed College, which along with most every other charitable and civic organization in early Portland, had been founded by Thomas Lamb Eliot, the church's first minister. The public library, the art museum, the Boys and Girls Club, the Humane Society— all had begun with the vision of Eliot and his congregants.

I had done my homework, and I knew that the church had been on hold for the past few years. The former minister had lost two wives to cancer in the last five years of his ministry, losses that had greatly affected him, as well as the congregation. A sadness prevailed. The church needed new life.

The search committee was what one might expect: three mature women, who were church leaders, a youngish city bureaucrat, an older lawyer, a stockbroker, and a young adult. My conviction that this was the church I was called to grew during the initial interview. I realized that First Unitarian was ready to flower, and I felt my heart open: I wanted to be in Portland, and I wanted to be with these people. I thought that I could provide the leadership they needed for their next phase. As the interview was winding down, I waited for the right moment, a silence that provoked attention. I looked at the committee members and said plainly, This is where I am called to be.

My declaration was premature, of course—moreover, a unilateral one and not mine to make. Since I was the second out of five candidates in a nationwide search, the committee members looked around at one another and coughed politely. Finally one of the women asked, What makes you think so?

My response rolled off my tongue. After all, the words had been waiting two years to be spoken. I can offer you some things that you need, I said. I'm a strong preacher, and a large church needs a strong preacher. I paused, and then went on. More important, you are a great church, and you have forgotten this. I can help you remember that you are great. I paused again, to let my promise sink in, then I continued. And you can give me something I need: I need to be challenged to excellence, and you can do that for me.

I delivered my pre-candidating sermon at University Unitarian in Seattle that Sunday. I had been warned by my mentor, John Buehrens, to preach a "safe" sermon: Don't say anything that would make anyone on the committee want to reject you, he said. I didn't take his advice. Quite honestly, I can't recall the title, but I do remember the topic: I preached on the relationship between spirituality and the erotic. I thought that if the committee chose me, they should know what they were getting.

Just before I entered the sanctuary, one of the committee members, Florence Rawson—now dead with a stroke—called my attention to a nondescript bush near the sanctuary. When I looked, she said, There's your little bird. Sure enough, there was a little brown bird sitting amidst the branches.

Two months later, the chair of the search committee called to tell me I had been selected. The candidating week went well, and the vote was 94.7% positive, as I remember. A minister hopes for 98 or 99% in the congregational vote, but I was the first female senior minister called to the church, and a group of long-time members quite frankly didn't want me. I didn't look like a minister to them, and I didn't sound like one, with my soft voice and Southern accent. Led by a member of the search committee, they lobbied against me. But the rest of the congregation was willing to take a chance on me. I accepted the call.

I had assumed that because of my Southern background, I would be called to a church in the Southeast. I thought Southeast, God said Northwest: I had been called to a place where the very topography was intimidating. Whenever I met someone new, he or she would ask, Do you cycle? Do you hike? Do you ski? Growing up in the South, I certainly didn't ski—in fact, I hadn't seen snow before I did graduate work at the University of Arkansas at Fayetteville. There were no hiking trails in the stubby pines of North Louisiana, and I had stopped riding a bike at age sixteen. I was daunted by this audacious new land and its athletic occupants.

At the same time, I understood that I had arrived at exactly the right place. This was not the Northeast, where people ask you where you went to boarding school. This was not the South, where family counted above all. This was not the Midwest, steeped in strong values, but unable to imagine new ways. No, this was the Left Coast, where anything was possible, where the only relevant question is: Do you have the right stuff?

The installation service was at the First Methodist Church because our sanctuary was not large enough for the event. It was a grand occasion, attended by the mayor, the president of Reed College, and various dignitaries from the denomination. My sons Kash and Madison were there that evening, in their suits, all grown up. My work had taken me from them. That evening, they came to witness and to celebrate what their sacrifice had yielded.

Needless to say, I had a lot to learn about ministry. My challenges were complicated by the rapid growth of the congregation. Early in my ministry—in fact, before I ever stepped into the pulpit—we wrapped the church block with a red ribbon and declared ourselves a Hate Free Zone, as a witness against a state ballot measure seeking to overturn the civil rights of gays and lesbians.* Local media featured the story, and First Unitarian became the go-to church not only for gays and lesbians, but for liberals who had been unchurched, but searching spiritually. The congregation grew forty per cent my first year in Portland.

Overwhelmed, I became radically dependent upon the God that brought me to Portland. If I was truly called, I knew I would be held. And I was held during all of my seventeen years of ministry there in Portland.

᪥

---

* Wrapping the block was the idea of Kathy Oliver, the Executive Director of Outside In, a social service agency that had long rented from First Unitarian. Outside In served runaway teens, many of whom left home because their sexual orientation had been found unacceptable by their parents.

I knew I would not be ministering alone. I was partnered with the Spirit that brought me to this church and that had sustained me through the years. I brought little experience as a minister, but I brought all that time had wrought. I brought my years of study in education, English, and social work. I brought my work as a teacher and psychotherapist and writer. I brought my learning as a wife, as a mother, as a lover and as a friend. And perhaps more significant than any of that, I brought the questions and doubts and the pain that flowed through the years I had lived. I put all of me on the altar. *All that is within me.* Redemption is possible, I knew.

The scripture promises "those who seek will find." Yes, we will find—but not necessarily what we think we want. And maybe not on our own timeline. Or in the way we expect. Or in the place we think. And every decision has its costs, for ourselves and for others. But we follow the thread.

I had found my call at last. I had come home. I was fifty years old and ready to begin.

CHAPTER 64

in which I rest, and am thankful

THE FIRST SNOW OF WINTER IS HERE, BIG SHEETS OF IT ARE WAFTING down. Looks like it's going to stay for a while. It is my first winter in Portland, where I am told the climate is mild, but there is a foot and half of snow on the ground.

The cold is much greater than last week, and I can't seem to get warm. My hands feel stiff and dry as I write, sitting here at my computer. I chafe my knuckles to warm them. My body tightens, and the chill moves from my hands and feet inward, towards my center. My work draws me, though, and my fingers begin to warm and loosen as the words of my sermon appear. This sermon is tricky—it's for the first Sunday of the New Year. I finally relax and allow the cold its proper place. I take a break, make a cup of steaming hot tea. As I sip the tea, a fantasy eases its way into my consciousness, unasked for and barely acknowledged: the fantasy of a spiritual partner I might come upon and love. It is the young girl's secret dream of the wedding lace still alive, close inside, like a wish too precious and fragile to tell. I want to go back and do it all over again, this time passionately, perfectly. My grieving is not yet complete. I wonder if it ever is, for anyone.

I smile at myself as I sit there with my hands cradling the cup, wanting the warmth. I cannot be younger than I am, and love is not deliverance anymore. I don't know what to expect, or even what to want. I feel the solidness under me, of the floor, of the chair, supporting me. This moment, at least, is palpable and I feel content, thankful, in the midst of it.

That night, the sermon done, I retreat to my bath. I rest, my head lying on the back of the tub, the water soothing, warming me through, down to my fingertips and toes. *Yes, I would like to be with a man again, when the time seems right. If the time ever seems right. I'm in no hurry. I have my church, good work to do.* My fingers flutter over the surface of the water, and my shoulders sink below. The bath is warm. *It's good, the warmth of the water. This is a fine, full moment of resting.*

I give thanks, and turn away from my thoughts. I know that more will be revealed.

Photos

First Communion – Marilyn at 6

Family Picture – Marilyn at 9

Marilyn's Father

High School Graduation

Granny and Big Papa

Wedding Day

At Home in Lexington

Madison, Marilyn and Kash in Berkeley

CPSIA information can be obtained at www.ICGtesting.com
Printed in the USA
BVOW05s0927210714

359465BV00001B/23/P

9 780615 955384